Little Girl Lost

THE AZRIELI SERIES OF HOLOCAUST SURVIVOR MEMOIRS: PREVIOUSLY PUBLISHED TITLES

ENGLISH TITLES

TITRES FRANÇAIS

Little Girl Lost

Betty Rich

THE AZRIELI FOUNDATION
www.azrielifoundation.org

Cover and book design by Mark Goldstein
Endpaper maps by Martin Gilbert
Inside maps by François Blanc
Family tree by Keaton Taylor

LIBRARY AND ARCHIVES CANADA CATALOGUING IN PUBLICATION

Rich, Betty, 1923–
        Little girl lost/ Betty Rich.

(The Azrieli series of Holocaust survivor memoirs. Series IV)
Includes bibliographical references and index.
ISBN 978-1-897470-25-1

1. Rich, Betty, 1923–. 2. Holocaust, Jewish (1939–1945) – Poland – Personal narratives. 3. Jewish women in the Holocaust – Poland – Biography. 4. Jewish women in the Holocaust – Soviet Union – Biography. 5. Holocaust survivors – Canada – Biography. 6. Polish Canadians – Biography. I. Azrieli Foundation. II. Title. III. Series: Azrieli series of Holocaust survivor memoirs. Series IV

DS134.72.R53A3 2011   940.53'18092   C2011-902619-8

MIX
From responsible sources
FSC® C004191

PRINTED IN CANADA

The Azrieli Series of Holocaust Survivor Memoirs

Contents

Series Preface: In their own words. . .

In telling these stories, the writers have liberated themselves. For so many years we did not speak about it, even when we became free people living in a free society. Now, when at last we are writing about what happened to us in this dark period of history, knowing that our stories will be read and live on, it is possible for us to feel truly free. These unique historical documents put a face on what was lost, and allow readers to grasp the enormity of what happened to six million Jews – one story at a time.

David J. Azrieli, C.M., C.Q., M.Arch
Holocaust survivor and founder, The Azrieli Foundation

Since the end of World War II, over 30,000 Jewish Holocaust survivors have immigrated to Canada. Who they are, where they came from, what they experienced and how they built new lives for themselves and their families are important parts of our Canadian heritage. The Azrieli Foundation's Holocaust Survivor Memoirs Program was established to preserve and share the memoirs written by those who survived the twentieth-century Nazi genocide of the Jews of Europe and later made their way to Canada. The program is guided by the conviction that each survivor of the Holocaust has a remarkable story to tell, and that such stories play an important role in education about tolerance and diversity.

Millions of individual stories are lost to us forever. By preserving the stories written by survivors and making them widely available to a broad audience, the Azrieli Foundation's Holocaust Survivor Memoirs Program seeks to sustain the memory of all those who perished at the hands of hatred, abetted by indifference and apathy. The personal accounts of those who survived against all odds are as different as the people who wrote them, but all demonstrate the courage, strength, wit and luck that it took to prevail and survive in such terrible adversity. The memoirs are also moving tributes to people – strangers and friends – who risked their lives to help others, and who, through acts of kindness and decency in the darkest of moments, frequently helped the persecuted maintain faith in humanity and courage to endure. These accounts offer inspiration to all, as does the survivors' desire to share their experiences so that new generations can learn from them.

The Holocaust Survivor Memoirs Program collects, archives and publishes these distinctive records and the print editions are available free of charge to libraries, educational institutions and Holocaust-education programs across Canada, and at Azrieli Foundation educational events. They are also available for sale to the general public at bookstores. All editions of the books are available for free download on our web site at: www.azrielifoundation.org.

The Azrieli Foundation would like to express appreciation to the following people for their invaluable efforts in producing this series: Simone Abrahamson, Florence Buathier, Darrel Dickson (Maracle Press), Sir Martin Gilbert, Stan Greenspan, Arnaud Regnaud, Sylwia Szymańska-Smolkin, Keaton Taylor, Robert Jan van Pelt, Lise Viens, Margie Wolfe and Emma Rodgers of Second Story Press, and Piotr Wróbel.

About the Glossary

The following memoir contains a number of terms, concepts and historical references that may be unfamiliar to the reader. For information on major organizations; significant historical events and people; geographical locations; religious and cultural terms; and foreign-language words and expressions that will help give context and background to the events described in the text, please see the glossary beginning on page 177.

Introduction

If I close my eyes, I see a movie. I see myself as a little girl; I see the sadness in my eyes. I still look after that little girl today. She never grew up. She's still there, waiting and hoping and always so alone. She's a part of me that is so lost and confused. So I enter the movie theatre of my life and try to put together scattered fragments, like a documentary, and take the little girl out into the open. I follow her across continents, through the trials and tribulations of World War II and through miraculous events of survival, when the cruel and harsh reality of everyday life was so overwhelming that it didn't take much to break down. She survived in a strange land and a strange culture, all alone.

In this poetic passage Betty Rich ponders the challenges of finding the form and language in which to tell her Holocaust story and to reflect on its meanings in her life after liberation. More than forty years after her many experiences escaping from the Nazis, she composes an elegiac reflection that moves between "I" and "She," and so positions herself throughout her memoir as character, narrator and commentator. Looking back onto the past and into herself, she recreates her odyssey through World War II as both testimony and a meditation on what it meant to her sense of self to endure and survive. Born Basia Kohn in June 1923, Rich writes her story of growing up in pre-war Poland and escape into the Soviet Union as a montage of graphic snapshots and moments in motion. Interwoven into her memories of events and people is her powerful longing to understand the dual sense of self created by her experiences both as a child within her family and community and as a young woman growing into adulthood in exile. Recounting the story of her first twenty-six years offers the welcome opportunity to provide a coherent structure to the chaotic events that engulfed her and those with whom she escaped from the Nazi invasion of Poland into Soviet labour camps.

In addition to historical documentation and a reflective form of narrative, Rich's memoir offers testimony that reveals the psychological pressures on survival and its aftermath. We find the beginnings of this aftermath in Rich's decision to close her memoir with reflections and portions of letters about the new and complicated beginnings of her life in Canada. Here, along with the challenges of adaptation to a new language and culture, she summarizes her encounters and initial impressions of the Toronto Jewish community and their social habits as a complicated "wonderland." The brevity of this conclusion concentrates our attention on her experience of survival, with its ominous but riveting adventures across an unknown continent, emotional isolation, and intense intimate relationships. Her narrative of five years from the frozen north to the warm climes of Georgia in the Soviet Union also represents a belated coming of age story where despite or perhaps because of physical and emotional suffering, Basia Kohn experienced a voyage of self discovery and self-determination. It is this legacy along with the rich complexity of her portrait of her childhood and family that she offers to her children, grandchildren and her wider audience.

Basia had already revealed her talent and drive to write in the diaries she kept since childhood. As she looks back from the perspective of her moment of escape in 1939 when she was sixteen, she creates a multilayered perspective that shows us her process of remembering. She uses fragments of her memory to recreate a complex portrait of her childhood in the city of Zduńska Wola, a town of textile manufacturing in central Poland, of about 20,000 people, and located forty kilometres southwest of the city of Lodz. She then interlaces her developing awareness of relationships within her family as they intersect with the local Jewish community. At the same time she recognized the economic and political forces that shaped the dynamics of these relationships as they unfolded. Her memoir continues by following the chronology of her cross continental travels, from the fears of the Nazi presence in Poland to privation in labour camps and moments and places of reprieve. Rich's memoir is punctuated by harrowing coincidences and personal and political treachery as well as fortuitous encounters that led to loving and supportive relationships.

Writing from her home in Toronto some forty years after the war's end encourages Betty Rich to reflect on whether it is possible for her and her readers to understand the events that engulfed her. Also threaded throughout the memoir and reconsidered in her Epilogue are her reflections on such philosophical questions about relationships among events that appeared to be her fated destiny, her impulsive and self-conscious choices, and the question of whether change is possible under the pressures of crisis and catastrophe. The resulting memoir combines artistry and analysis in an interweave of questions, reflections and detailed story of five years of physical and emotional survival in the Soviet Union and return to Poland. The result is a significant contribution to study of the Holocaust.

The incidents and relationships that define Betty Rich's childhood in Zduńska Wola also engage us with a world that may be lost to us but is also strikingly familiar in its economic vicissitudes and rich and complicated panorama of social, religious and family relations. The Kohn family typified the complexity of Jewish life in interwar Poland. Along with modernization, the rise of Polish nationalism and constitutional guarantees against discrimination, intolerance of minorities like the Jews intensified. Despite centuries of the Jews' economic and cultural contributions, this was a time when prejudice increased to the point of overwhelming intolerance. Poland was celebrating its own political independence, national culture and economic growth and the Jews were seen as usurping the professional, business and government work that rightfully belonged to Poles. Rich presents Zduńska Wola, a small provincial city, as a microcosm of these developments. The vibrant presence of various Jewish religious and political beliefs and activities resonates with the complicated political and economic experiences of Jewish life throughout twentieth-century Poland before 1939. The Jews of Poland had always been subject to populist and official persecution and attacks, and had historically been segregated into such occupations as commerce, money lending and collecting. Nonetheless, they were also able to apply their skills to find economic success in the textile industry in which Basia's father had a small factory and to which the Kohn family owed its short lived prosperity. Just as Rich's reflections alternate between "I" and "She," so she narrates the changing economic fortunes of her family as oscillating between security and displacement. Her "I" reflects the economic impact on her developing self as she recreates her childhood "She" as buffeted between feeling loved and feeling distanced from her family.

The Kohn parents and children also represent the confluence of a variety of Jewish religious and political identities and practices within Poland's urban Jewish population. Although Basia's parents were both Orthodox in background and observance, her father represents a strong tie to religious tradition mixed with adaptation to modernity. He had been educated both as a rabbi in the Hasidic branch of Orthodox Judaism characterized by joyous spiritualism and tutored in secular subjects. As they grew to maturity, Basia's four brothers made different decisions to free themselves from the strictures of Orthodox Judaism. They each affiliated with different Jewish organizations, ranging from the politically socialist left to the General Zionist Organization to the religious Agudath Israel. Fulfilling his own Zionist commitment, Basia's older brother Motek immigrated to pre-state Israel.

Basia found an intellectual and social home in joining Hashomer Hatzair, a socialist Zionist youth movement that was founded immediately before World War I in Central Europe. Committed to a secular Jewish culture, the movement appealed to Jewish youth seeking a way of combining a strong Jewish identity with a progressive egalitarian ideology that would include such Zionist values as peace and social justice. The movement introduced young Jews to the Hebrew language, ancient and modern Jewish history, and emphasized athletics. Through camping and other group activities, Hashomer Hatzair also cultivated leadership and non-competitive relationships that would support a self-determining and vigorous community of youth and the creation of collectively owned kibbutz settlements in British Mandatory Palestine and hopefully, eventually in a Jewish State. Although Basia's adoption of a secular Jewish identity and culture was in clear opposition to her father's Orthodox beliefs and observances, upon witnessing Hashomer Hatzair's activities for himself, he acquiesced. Rich's portrait of her father is not only complex, but shows how his commitment to Orthodox attitudes and change of heart reflect the influence of secular movements on the observance of religious traditions. It was also Hashomer Hatzair that inspired and formed some of the group of youngsters with whom Basia Kohn would escape to the Soviet Union.

Despite their differences, all branches of Zionism shared the belief in creating a self-determining Jewish nation in the historic homeland of biblical Israel with which the Jewish people identified as its place of origin. In addition to ideological, religious and historical identification, it was hoped that a Jewish state would provide protection from their ongoing oppression in Europe. Not all Jews of Central Europe were Zionists, however. The Bund, a non-Zionist Jewish socialist movement prominent in Poland, Russia, and Lithuania, notably celebrated secular European Jewish culture by identifying and expressing it through the Yiddish language as opposed to Hebrew.

Conflicting political and religious allegiances, intergenerational

misunderstandings, and the roller-coaster effects of economic instability, including economic depression, led to constant change to
which Basia's family constantly adapted. Rich's memoir dramatizes
these changes in a series of vignettes that intimately portray the effects on members of her family. The challenges faced by the Kohn
family ranged from economic necessity and individual ambition and
desire for self-determination to the religiously prescribed roles for
women and men. When her father falls ill and is unable to conduct
his business and support the family, out of necessity, her mother must
enter this public sphere. Through Rich's dramatically detailed rendering, we recognize the transformation of lives governed by tradition
into modernity. When Basia's mother discards the wig required as a
head-covering for Orthodox women, we see the power of a woman's
modern determination to meld public and private roles. Ultimately,
however, the struggle to sustain progress and maintain family and
community stability was forced to yield to the Nazis' obsession to
destroy Jewish community, culture and identity.

Of course the greatest anxiety of her childhood overwhelmed
even economic hardship. As Rich documents, although Poland had
suffered various occupations over the centuries, escaping the Nazis
was difficult to impossible. In addition to successive bureaucratic de-
lays in issuing exit visas, entry visas to safe countries were not only
severely limited in number, but required costly payments for documentation, economic guarantees and sponsorship from the country of emigration. Family responsibilities such as caring for elderly
and sick parents and grandparents kept others from leaving. After
September 1939, when Germany invaded Poland, the exits shut down.
From 1939 through 1941, about 300,000 out of Poland's 3,000,000
Polish Jews took the precipitous risk of making their way through
and around the Nazi occupying forces into the Soviet Union, which
in agreement with Germany, had taken over the eastern regions of
Poland. Some like Basia and her friends were helped by guides to
cross the border even though they had no way of knowing if the

guide was friend or foe or exactly where they were going. Although the Soviets had no extermination plans or concentration camps, as officials learned of the presence of Jewish refugees, they sent most of them into the vast reaches of Siberia, Central Asia and beyond. Despite horrific conditions in labour camps and other settlements, including starvation, disease, lack of medical care and adequate clothing in the frozen north or arid regions of Central Asia, most of them managed to survive. When the Germans invaded the Soviet Union in June 1941, more than a million Russian Jews and refugees managed to reach Soviet Central Asia and therefore save themselves from Nazi extermination. All together, the Jews who survived in the Soviet Union also represent the largest group of European Jews to survive the Nazi onslaught against them.

Although Rich's story is crucial to the history and experience of the Holocaust, it takes place far away from the ghettos, concentration camps and death centres whose searing images have become icons of Nazi atrocities and the suffering they produced. And yet there is no doubt, as her memoir conveys so clearly, that the story of survival in the Soviet Union not only adds to but illuminates our knowledge of the Holocaust. At the end of December 1939, four months after Poland was invaded by Germany, sixteen-year-old Basia left her family home in Zduńska Wola. Her hope was to escape an uncertain future; in fact, she escaped incarceration and death at the hands of the Nazis. Along with a group of other young people, she embarked on a journey that would take them across the Polish border north eastward into the Soviet Union to an unknown destination where they hoped they would find safe harbour. Over the next five years, a meandering and bewildering succession of trains carried them over 4,000 kilometres, first to the village of Kuźnica, about fifty kilometres from Bialystok, whose farmers and Jewish tradesmen lived in economic interdependence. This was to become Rich's first home in the Soviet Union until she and her friends were deported to a labour camp near Arkhangelsk, surrounded by thousands of miles of dense forest even further north than Siberia. Under constant surveillance, despite their lack of bodily strength and training, they were assigned the work of felling and splitting timber. But amidst difficult conditions, including lack of sufficient and nutritious food, the onset of frostbite, and lack of medical care, old and new friendships offered solace. As so many Holocaust memoirs confirm, close, trusting and supportive relationships offered emotional and social sustenance that in turn motivated prisoners to go on another day and even envision a normal future life. *Little Girl Lost* is filled with moments of closeness that, as she and friends shared their pain, provided that emotional sustenance. Reminiscences of ordinary, happy times, sharing food and physical help as well as songs and even laughter filled in the years of suffering that should have been a time of individual development enhanced by community involvement.

It was the Soviet Union's most dire moment in World War II that brought hope to Basia and her friends. When Germany launched Operation Barbarossa and attacked the USSR in June 1941, Basia's group was granted permission to leave the Arkhangelsk camp. The Soviets were not prepared for the invasion because they had signed a non-aggression treaty with Germany in 1939, known as the Molotov-Ribbentrop pact, in which each nation promised not to attack the other. Hitler, however, always considered the agreement a temporary measure to give Germany time to conquer Western Europe. He had a greater priority. He had always planned to destroy the USSR along with its Jews. Consistent with Nazi racialist ideology, the Jews were part of a larger "Jewish-Bolshevik conspiracy" that had subjugated the Soviet Union and if not destroyed would rival the Nazis for world conquest. Nazi ideology also considered the Jews as subhuman and as representing the fundamentally degenerate racial character of the Soviet Union. As the invasion pushed forward, among other tasks assigned to the Einsatzgruppen – mobile killing units that were part of the Security Police – was to identify and organize the execution of those who could mount resistance attacks against the German forces and those who opposed German supremacy in Eastern Europe. The primary targets of the Einsatzgruppen were Jewish men, Communist officials, and the Roma and Sinti people of the Soviet Union. As testing ground for what would become the Final Solution, the killing occurred so quickly and on such a massive scale that few ghettos and other encampments were built to incarcerate the Soviet Jews before they were killed. Only by the middle of November 1942 was the Red Army able to stop the German advance in central Russia. The climactic and decisive battle occurred in Stalingrad, where after two months of fierce combat and incalculable casualties on both sides, the German army, suffering from the intense cold, surrendered and its invasion was over by February 1943. The Soviet military then pushed back and by the end of 1943 had almost reclaimed Russia and large parts of the Ukraine and Belorussia. Not until 1944 did the Red Army reconquer all of European Russia.

During the entire period of the German invasion, while fear and despair were visible on the faces of the Soviet people, actual information about the battles was sparse and vague due to censorship. News also served as propaganda about the progress of the war. Ironically, while the news of Germany's invasion of the Soviet Union was devastating to most of the populace, for Basia and her friends it was a fortuitous event. With permission to travel anywhere, they picked Staliniri, named after Joseph Stalin. A new city in the state of South Ossetia, part of the republic of Georgia with its own ethnic identity and culture, Staliniri is located on the Black Sea, 3,000 kilometres from Arkhangelsk. Staliniri meant relief from unbearable cold and privation and possibilities for a decent life with paid work. Staliniri was bombed by the Germans in 1942 and although there was little damage, it reminded Basia and her friends that their escape from Nazi persecution could not be guaranteed and might be only momentary. If the Germans had succeeded in conquering and occupying the USSR, the indigenous and refugee Jews would have been killed. It was only with the Soviet counteroffensive that news began to be broadcast and Basia and her group of Polish refugees could take temporary solace in the immediate danger having passed. The last stop in Basia's odyssey through the Soviet Union was the city of Kutaisi, further south in Georgia, where she worked in a makeshift workshop organized by her friends, handcrafting sewing thread. Although they were harassed by the N K V D, the Soviet Secret Police, Basia remained there until the end of the war when she felt compelled to return to Poland to look for her family.

Upon arriving in Lodz, Basia learned how Jews had been transported from all over Poland, including from her home town, to join the local Jews as they were forced into a ghetto. Created in February 1940, the walled off dilapidated area of Lodz isolated about 160,000 people from the rest of the population in unbearably crowded and unsanitary conditions. Whether these conditions were designed to eliminate them with disease and starvation is a subject of scholarly debate. Those who remained alive and even resistant to this oppression were mostly deported to forced labour and concentration camps as well as killing centres. Among the remarkable examples of ghetto resistance were, despite prohibition, the effort to record individual experiences and observations in writing and the establishment of underground schools, synagogues and performing centres. Where books were confiscated, literary discussion groups sprang up. Musical performances in makeshift cabarets satisfied other cravings for cultural expression. But while Jewish culture, and through it, hope, was sustained in the isolated captivity of the Lodz ghetto, the Germans used this isolation to enforce an insidious plan to keep the Jews from learning any information about their dark future. The transports from Lodz began in January 1942 and when the ghetto was obliterated in August 1944, death awaited nearly all of its prisoners.

Among the many compelling elements of *Little Girl Lost* is the candour with which Rich writes about her own struggle for self-determination within her family and community, where she always felt different. Her narration of incidents from her past is interwoven with commentary that shows how despite deep differences, her current life in Canada resonates with feelings and moments from her childhood in Poland. Her memoir is shaped by the intersections of past and present, showing us how her responses in the present interact with her recreation of the past to build a narrative memorial to her lost family life. While her life has been defined by constant change and adaptations, she discovers and examines how it has also retained elements that she identifies as core characteristics. She recalls that in elementary school she responded to the mix of rich and poor children and their unequal treatment by demanding that everyone be treated the same. While she does not remember the teacher's response, she acknowledges that speaking out became a trait that could work for better or worse. It was in school that Basia recognized her growing curiosity about the world around her and desire to explore, experiment and be noticed. Rich's memoir can thus be read as a chronicle of personal exploration into possibilities for making choices. It also reveals how the historical and political constraints enforced by the Holocaust affected her drive for self-determination. As the economic depression reduced the Kohn family's circumstances and Basia was unable to continue in school past the age of fourteen, she learned to adapt to change by recognizing it as a welcome challenge to her intellectual and social development. Although her own secular beliefs create an ideological break from her father's Orthodoxy, she recalls how the family's celebration of Jewish holidays remains among the happiest memories of her childhood. The festive meals, shared rituals and singing created an atmosphere of tranquility that would banish the anxieties of economic instability and constant threats of poverty. Looking back from the present, Rich describes her celebrations of Jewish holidays in Toronto as incorporating those memories of her Polish childhood and thus shows us how celebration becomes memorialisation for this survivor.

Rich's narrative is interspersed with letters from her mother to fill in the gaps she cannot remember. The letters also highlight the struggle we find in so many Holocaust memoirs to find the precise language with which to communicate the deadly realities victims and survivors faced. Interspersing her mother's letters and postcards with her own narration provides us with primary documentation of this struggle as well as the fears and responses to the terrors both women experienced. In addition to fears and realities of censorship, neither mother nor daughter, each beset with her own privations, wanted to upset and endanger the other with the details of her suffering. Without knowing any details of the other's experiences, however, it is clear from the letters that mother and daughter felt one another's anxiety and therefore each one was driven to imagine the worst. The complexity of this written and unspoken dialogue offers a form of analysis that encourages us to approach Holocaust experiences and responses from the perspective of victims and survivors and learn how they would like us to understand them. When the letters and postcards from Basia's mother come to an end, we see how the daughter's anxieties about her mother's fate must remain suspended until she can return to Poland. What she learns, however, can never relieve this anxiety, for the Jewish community of Zduńska Wola was deported to the Lodz ghetto and then to the camps and killing centres. Like so many survivors, Basia returned to find that she had lost almost all of her family.

Among the many illuminating features of Betty Rich's memoir is its graphically complex picture of how traumatic suffering becomes part of the fabric of everyday life in the Holocaust. In their relentless repetition, unthinkable conditions become the expected, not the extraordinary. And yet, even in the narration of intensely detailed moments of physical threats to survival and personal betrayal, the memoir is always reflective. Such reflection applies to Rich's demonstration that the extraordinary did occur in random acts of kindness, emotional and material generosity and in the discovery of love and friendship. Within her narration of sometimes harsh conditions, Rich interweaves encounters that expose underlying compassion, as in her meeting with an NKVD bureaucrat who, even in his willingness to hear her story, risks his own position and freedom. The dramatic rendering with which Rich's memoir narrates such encounters and characterizations creates a complex picture that brings to life the people and places that made survival for the Jews possible as they both suffered yet found compassion.

Phyllis Lassner
Northwestern University
2011

SOURCES

Adelson, Alan and Robert Lapides. *Łódz Ghetto: Inside a Community under Siege.* New York: Viking 1989.
"Invasion of the Soviet Union." *Holocaust Encyclopedia*, United States Holocaust Memorial Museum. http://www.ushmm.org/wlc/en/article.php?ModuleId=10005164
Mendelsohn, Ezra and Isaiah Trunk. "Poland," in *Encylopaedia Judaica*, 2nd Edition, vol.16, ed. Fred Skolnik. New York: Macmillan, 2006.

Betty Rich's Family Tree*

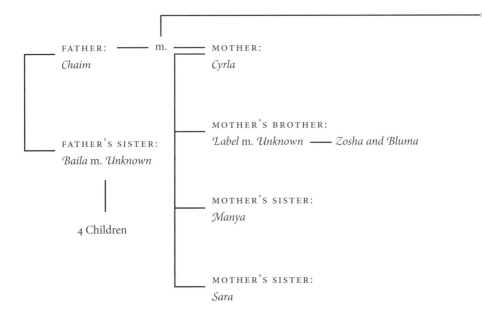

FATHER: —— m. —— **MOTHER:**
Chaim   *Cyrla*

MOTHER'S BROTHER:
Label m. *Unknown* —— *Zosha and Bluma*

FATHER'S SISTER:
Baila m. *Unknown*

MOTHER'S SISTER:
Manya

4 Children

MOTHER'S SISTER:
Sara

BROTHER:
Mordechai (Motek) m. *Rachel* —— *Ciporah*

BROTHER:
Jacob (Yakov) m. *Lajka*

BROTHER:
Fishel

BROTHER:
Abram

SISTER:
Fela m. *Herman* (first husband)
      m. *Jacob* (second husband) —— *Pauline*

SON:
Chuck m. *Candace* —— *Rebecca*

—— *Sharyl*

*Betty (Basia) Kohn;
born 1923 m. *David Recht* ——

DAUGHTER:
Susan m. *Michael* —— *David*

—— *Ryan*

BROTHER:
Rafael (Fulek)

To my mother,
a woman of valour
who loved me unconditionally.

Author's Preface

To this day, when meeting new people, I am often asked where I originally come from, because of my quite obvious accent, and I always make them guess. After going through at least ten different countries in Europe or the Middle East, I reveal the answer and, invariably, they show great disappointment. I wonder why they are surprised. Did they expect something more exciting? What is wrong with coming from Poland?

For many years, I had my own reasons to not deal with where I came from and who I was. I have tried almost desperately not to remember. I knew a time would come when I would have to dig and dig and try very hard to put together my first sixteen years. I can't bury it forever. I have to free myself, to work at it like a jigsaw puzzle, piece by piece, to fit together whatever my memory can retrieve. I know it will be painful at times just to find the words to describe a feeling or a moment from so long ago.

When I returned to Poland immediately after the war, I was confronted with a tragic comedy being played out around me, a great celebration of life on top of the ashes of a great fire. There was also bitterness and rage, yet death had not conquered the living, the survivors. Self-reproach and guilt for being alive would only have devastated whatever little spark was left in us.

The premise that no one ever really dies because they can be resurrected through memories makes sense to me. When my daughter, Susan, was fourteen years old, a person very close to us died and she wrote, "I don't understand; I know I won't see her anymore, but in my mind, she will remain alive until my memory fades. Even so, I don't understand death. The body they bury means nothing to me. The funeral is only a symbol. It will not take her away. She will only be gone when all the people who knew her are dead."

And so I stumbled upon the real reason for my desire to put my story down on paper: I wanted to do it for my children's sake and for their children's, just in case my memory dies. I am the only one left who remembers my family, who remembers my particular story.

~

Throughout my life, my favourite expression whenever I was at a loss for words to describe an event was "I could write a book." Since early childhood, I kept some kind of a diary on and off; when the need to pour out my emotions was overwhelming, the weight too heavy to carry, I wrote about it.

I used to consider my need to understand what was going on around me and inside me, my need to find answers, a weakness. I was constantly probing, analyzing, forever searching in the darkness that seemed to envelop me most of the time. What, or who, was I looking for? In my long journey, I filled thousands of pages writing about experiences, feelings, people and places. I just wrote.

I know my life has not been an easy one, to say the least, but I thought that to feel the way I did was normal. I felt that so much of my pain was my fault and I even felt guilty about it. But I came to terms with the sadness and the pain of loneliness. I stopped questioning it. I accepted it. After trying to fight it, without any success, I gave up and just went about my life, whatever there was to it. That is, I stopped questioning it until I was thrown into one of the greatest crises in my life: the tragic loss of my husband, David, who drowned in 1971 while we were at a cottage in the Muskoka region.

I began to seek help and was told by one professional that my problems were from my childhood. He said that I should live for today and for tomorrow, that I needed to forget the past. But I know too well that the past is a prelude to the future, so I went to another doctor, Vivian Rakoff, who was then chief of psychiatry at Sunnybrook Hospital and shortly after became head of the famous Clarke Institute of Psychiatry (now called the Centre for Addiction and Mental Health). He really started me thinking on a different level. His first question was, "What can you tell me about your past?"

Remembering the other professional I had seen, I briefly related, in a very matter-of-fact tone, a few of the highlights of my life up until the loss of my husband. "Stop," he shouted. "What you have told me very briefly could shake up an army and you wonder why you feel the way you do? You could write a book about your life experiences up to now, up to the time that this new tragedy occurred."

In my talks with Dr. Rakoff, we never did begin to unravel my childhood or the turbulent years of being a teenager alone during the war. We had to apply first aid to the more recent wounds. But at least I no longer felt that I was just a complainer. I have reasons for being the way I am. I came to see that I had done a pretty good job of coping, and according to him, I even deserve a lot of credit and shouldn't feel guilty or ashamed about my very normal reactions.

Seventeen years have passed since the tragedy of my husband's accident. The idea of writing down my experiences had been haunting me for years – sometimes vaguely, sometimes acutely. I have been encouraged by my children, as well as by other people who just liked the way I expressed myself without even knowing what I had to write about, but I kept postponing for many reasons. Could I tell the full story of my life? Could I go back to my childhood? Some time ago I read a passage about childhood that has taken on a special significance for me. It talked about how all unsatisfied needs from childhood come up the rest of our lives; that all the pain and hurt we felt then would always be there unless we connected with someone we could tell about it or intuitively understood us so well that he or she was able to meet our emotional needs.

~

I was sixteen when the war broke out in 1939, and I know that I must begin by writing about my first sixteen years. For years, I tried to tell myself that I didn't remember them because after sixteen I entered a new stage of my life. Lately, however, something has given me the impetus, the courage to begin.

If I close my eyes, I see a movie. I see myself as a little girl; I see the sadness in my eyes. I still look after that little girl today. She never grew up. She's still there, waiting and hoping and always so alone. She's a part of me that is so lost and confused. So I enter the movie theatre of my life and try to put together scattered fragments, like a documentary, and take the little girl out into the open. I follow her across continents, through the trials and tribulations of World War II and through miraculous events of survival, when the cruel and harsh reality of everyday life was so overwhelming that it didn't take much to break down. She survived in a strange land and a strange culture, all alone.

Then she went back to where she was born, back to nothing, to nobody. What should have been a normal passage into a new life after the war became yet another journey of survival. Finally, I entered what some would call a stable period of twenty-one years, but even those times were not so peaceful for me.

The axe of fate struck again when my two children, a girl of sixteen and a boy of twenty, lost their father in a tragic drowning accident. And this little girl lost her Rock of Gibraltar, the only security she had ever had.

The next sixteen years alone were another period of transformation as I became a single woman, a widow. They were interesting years, but basically followed the same story. I was lonely most of the time, although I was also very successful in my new role. I tried hard to keep going, to survive.

Then, I began trying to find answers that would help the little girl inside me in her life-long struggle to understand herself. There is no one person to blame for all the things that happened to me, but at least through the process of writing this book I can see that one can't always be the master of one's destiny. At least I have the chance to look at myself and maybe even begin to like what I see. Maybe I will find out that I was brave, courageous, honest and, under many difficult circumstances, preserved my integrity.

Maybe, finally, after so many years, the woman I am today will begin to be proud of the little girl I was and accept her as part of her total being. Maybe, together, we will find some peace and contentment.

Betty Rich
1988

Beginnings

I was born on June 10, 1923, in Zduńska Wola, a town in central Poland, about forty kilometres southwest of the city of Lodz. When I was growing up, Zduńska Wola had a Jewish community of about 8,000 out of a total population of approximately 20,000. The town was largely made up of textile factories, which meant that we had an army of factory workers and factory owners, as well as all the regular services and stores. We lived at 27 ulica Kościelna (Church Street), named for the big church that happened to be just two blocks away from us. It was a mixed neighbourhood; as far as I recall, there were no particular divisions in our town. There were only poorer or richer streets, just like the world I live in today.

The building I lived in was a red-brick three-storey structure with a massive front gate facing Kościelna. Rising up on each side of the gate were two staircases that led to the flats upstairs. The gate itself opened into one large interior space that in turn led into a large courtyard enclosed on three sides by lower two-storey buildings. In one corner at the end of the courtyard was a fenced-in garden that belonged to our landlord who was of German descent. The garden is where I spent many beautiful hours with his little girl, Nelly, and her younger brother, Harry. I even learned some German from them. In the other back corner of the courtyard was the landlord's small sausage factory where pigs were slaughtered. In one of the front corners of the building, on one of the side streets, was their meat and sausage store; behind it were their living quarters. The main gate on Kościelna was locked for the night at eleven o'clock; after that you had to ring the superintendent to let you in if you forgot your key.

I was told by my older siblings that we used to occupy the whole second floor of our building and that the third floor had been my father's textile manufacturing plant. They showed me two big slabs in the ceiling of the gateway passage that opened for crates to be hauled up and down. But while I was growing up our family fortunes changed and our whole family – my parents and my six siblings – lived in just three rooms. I had four older brothers, Mordechai (Motek or Mordka), Yakov, Fishel and Abram, an older sister named Fela, and one younger brother named Rafael, although we called him Fulek. Our original flat had been divided down the middle and a Polish family – I remember them very distinctly – was living in the other half. Our three rooms consisted of a large kitchen, a combined living room and dining room, and another large room without any windows where I sometimes slept along with other members of my family.

My oldest brother, Motek, was red-haired with blue eyes. I remember him dragging around a saxophone since he played in the orchestra of the General Zionist organization. My second-oldest brother, Yakov, often played his violin and belonged to a different organization, the more religious Agudath Israel. Although my next two brothers, Fishel and Abram, played football on a Zionist organization team, they had begun to free themselves from the restrictions of religious Judaism and joined what they saw as the wave of the future, which meant being more to the left, more secular. My sister, Fela, also belonged to some kind of a Zionist group.[1] I was so much younger

1   For information on Zionist organizations, as well as on other major organizations; significant historical events and people; geographical locations; religious and cultural terms; and foreign-language words and expressions contained in the text, please see the glossary.

than my brothers that I don't remember where they worked; I was so young when my younger brother, Rafael, was born that I don't remember whether it affected my life.

My mother, Cyrla, was orphaned early in her life and was brought up by an aunt and uncle who came from a well-to-do Orthodox Jewish family – she was one of very few women of that era to have finished high school. She had dark hair and blue eyes, and owned several wigs because a religious Jewish woman always had to have her head covered. Sometimes she would wear a scarf or a different kind of head covering.

During my childhood I heard a lot about my mother's many wealthy relatives in Lodz. Some of them owned whole blocks of textile factories. I never met the very rich ones, but I remember my mother telling us that she used to visit them in Lodz and bring home their used clothes for us. My mother had one brother, Label, who lived in our town but he died when I was quite young and I don't remember him at all. I was in touch with his two older daughters, Zosha and Bluma, after the war. My mother also had two sisters in Lodz, Manya and Sara, who we kept in touch with, as well as their children. I had cousins, but being one of the youngest in my family, I didn't have much experience with being close to my extended family. My mother also had some cousins in Zduńska Wola; they were all quite well off by the standards of that time and place.

My father, Chaim Moshe, was very religious, Hasidic Orthodox, and he wore the clothes that signified that religious observance. He had a twin sister, Baila, and their parents – my grandparents – lived in a small town called Sieradz that was not far from Zduńska Wola. They owned both a vinegar and a soft drinks factory and were very respected and prosperous – they were held in high esteem by the Jewish community in the town. My father was educated in the Jewish religion and had the equivalent of a rabbinical diploma, which he never used. He had also been educated in secular subjects by private tutors – during his time, an Orthodox Jewish boy wasn't supposed to attend public school, where they might teach material that went counter to their religious upbringing. It was thought that public school would contaminate a child's mind with "foreign" matter. So if you were a poor, religious Jewish boy and you couldn't afford a tutor, you received only Jewish education and remained illiterate in other subjects.

My father's sister, who also lived in Sieradz, had four children. They were also well off in comparison to us. So as you can see, as a small girl, I already knew many people who lived differently than we did. Before I was born, my father got quite sick with some intestinal problems and due to both his illness and bad economic times (this was just before the Great Depression), his business affairs got progressively worse. My older brothers were involved in the family business and were able to get both a Jewish and private secular education before my family's wealth declined. My sister, Fela, who was six years older than me, was the first one of us to go to public school. She used to tell me that our family had maids before I was born and recalled many funny stories about some of them. She was more fortunate than me, being able to remember some good times. I had no such memories – I had to live with the reality of our poverty and tensions with regard to finances from early childhood.

My mother went into the family textile business and took over our accounts in Warsaw, where my father, who was not well enough to travel, used to sell the fabrics. She was away five days a week and would come home Thursday night to prepare for the Sabbath and then would leave again on Sunday.

As a little girl, I played with all the children in the neighbourhood. As I mentioned, I spent countless hours in our landlord's garden with his daughter, Nelly. For me, the garden was a dream world of beautiful flowers, vegetables and fruits that I could pick and eat. I played with Nelly a lot, but always at her house, never at mine. Very early on, I started to enjoy being away from my family and experiencing new foods and other things that were different from our traditions.

For instance, it was against the Jewish religion to eat pork or any non-kosher meat products, but I didn't care. When I was with Nelly's family I could get something I liked to eat and as much as I wanted of it. At home, there was never enough food to go around. I think that Nelly's parents liked having me around but it wasn't something that I took for granted – I was an insecure child who never felt confident that people liked me.

For reasons that I still don't fully understand, I never really felt part of my family. I loved them and I know that they loved me, but I was different and looked for experiences outside my family and their traditions. I also remember that I liked being sick because that was when I got their attention. I had bronchitis quite often, as well as all the other childhood diseases and, strangely enough, I loved those times. My parents would fuss over me and I could see how much they cared. No one in my family talked about love, and I didn't know what to expect from them. I grew like a wildflower, on my own. So, as I see it now, from an early age I tried to seek out nurturing elsewhere or, more precisely, I learned to survive.

I do remember some wonderful times with my parents on Saturday afternoons, a day of rest in every sense of the word, when they set aside all their worries and struggles and just relaxed. My father studied the Torah in the afternoon and I sometimes listened to him in bewilderment, an aura of mysticism around him. Later, my parents would take me for a walk in the meadows that stretched for miles not far from our house, where little creeks cut through. One creek had just a narrow thirty-centimetre-wide board across it and my father made me walk over it, saying, "Don't look down, just walk ahead, keep walking…." His voice still rings in my ears. I loved those walks; aside from the times when I was sick, they were the only times I felt part of the family.

I also remember the sad moments on Sunday afternoons in the summer when Nelly's family got into a horse and carriage and drove away to the countryside. There were no large bodies of fresh water in our town at all, so they would go to cottage areas where there were some rivers and lakes. I would stand and watch until they disappeared on the horizon, thinking, What a happy family, all dressed up in their best, with all their good food packed. I felt so left out. This feeling still persists. Sometimes I feel that everybody in the world is happy and has so much family, while I am so desolate and alone.

I have one particular memory of the wedding of one my parents' relatives, just before I was old enough to go to school. A dressmaker made me a beautiful off-white silk dress that had layers of wide ruffles in the skirt. And although I had no idea how I looked, after the wedding I got sick with a fever and my mother said it was because the people at the wedding had given me *ayin hora*, the "evil eye." It was an old Jewish superstition that an envious look could bring bad luck. I can only assume that I looked pretty, but mother never actually told me that.

These memories were all before I went to public school, which in Poland started at the age of seven and was compulsory and free for seven years. In Zduńska Wola, there were two public schools that were only for Jewish children; the rest took in children of other religions or nationalities. The children who went to those schools were mostly Polish, with some of German background and very few others. The two Jewish schools were located at opposite ends of town. One was in a poor, working class area where mainly Jews lived, and the other, where I went, was in my neighbourhood, a mixed part of the town that also had some very wealthy Jewish families. I was enrolled there thanks to fortunate timing in the life of our family – although we were already poor when I started school, we still lived in the same place. By that time, my oldest brother, Motek, had immigrated to pre-state Israel and my sister had finished her first seven years of school. Since she wasn't able to continue her education, she was sent to some rich relatives in Gdansk, a port on the Baltic Sea. She helped out in the relatives' business; I think they had some kind of store.

So, at that point, we were only five children at home. My school was in the middle of the most beautiful part of the city and was within walking distance from our building. Of course, at that time, everywhere we went was within walking distance. Although one could hire some very nice carriages (like taxis here), they were expensive. There were some cars around, but I never drove in one and I don't know who they belonged to.

The school was a three-storey building surrounded by a wrought-iron fence. The teachers could be either Jewish or Polish, but we had mostly Jewish teachers. For national Polish holidays, when we had very formal celebrations and gatherings, girls had to wear navy-blue pleated skirts and white blouses. For gymnastics, instead of shorts we wore navy-blue bloomers with elastic at both the waist and at the thighs, along with white tops. Although this was not a private school, the dress code was very rigid.

My first few days in school were very memorable. I immediately noticed that the girls and boys from the wealthy families looked different. They looked so pampered and clean. Our school uniform was a black dress of some sort – it could have buttons down the front or have pockets and could be made from various fabrics. Some were more stylish, some less. You had to have a white collar that was the same shape as the black collar so you could take it off and wash it. I remember that some of the girls had beautiful uniforms and right there began the separation by background, by your family's financial status. The boys also had to wear a uniform – theirs was black pants with a jacket.

It was at school that my encounter with a world different than mine began, and it was very dramatic. I started my struggle to be part of them, to almost push away who I was and where I lived (perhaps wrongly, but this was a fact). After a few days at school, I noticed that the teacher was favouring some pretty girls from well-to-do, prestigious families. Without talking to my mother or anyone else, I walked up to her when she was alone after school and said in a calm, serious voice, "Teacher, my mother told me to tell you that it's not fair to favour some children; everybody should be treated the same." She was astonished and I don't even remember what she replied – it didn't matter to me as long as I had said what I felt and what I was thinking. That's a character trait that I have used throughout my life, sometimes to my benefit, other times to my detriment.

I went to school six days a week – we had Saturdays off, unlike the Polish schools that had Sundays off. School started at eight o'clock in the morning and lasted for four hours, with a ten-to-fifteen-minute intermission. The younger grades went home at twelve or one, but from Grade 4 and up we stayed until two or three in the afternoon because we had more subjects to study. Twelve o'clock was time for lunch, which we brought from home; we could get drinks such as juice or milk at school. And here, again, I have a seemingly small recollection: the wealthy kids' lunches were different from mine – they had beautiful rolls filled with salmon or sardines, which were very expensive, as well as bananas, grapes and other fruits that didn't grow in Poland and were a luxury. They sometimes gave me part of their lunch; I was always eager to eat something different. My campaign to be liked by them and accepted began immediately.

Somehow I managed to squeeze myself into the homes and lives of the well-off girls and boys. Some weren't as wealthy as others, but I think I was at the bottom of the ladder. They had big six- or seven-room flats, with maids and beautiful furniture. It was a different world. Some of their parents were religious Jews, owners of big textile factories, and others were professionals such as doctors and lawyers. Soon I was practically living in their homes, but they never came over to mine. Was I jealous of them? I never thought about it. I took our differences as a fact of life. I didn't understand it but I accepted it and followed my natural instinct to do what was necessary to better my existence under the circumstances. In retrospect, I think that my friends' parents knew who my parents were and they knew the reasons for our financial downfall. They accepted me because I came from "good stock."

I also got the attention of the teachers. I was a good student and they seemed to like me – whenever the teachers needed someone to help them carry our notebooks to their homes, I was often picked to do it by almost every teacher. They usually asked me in and I spent hours visiting them. Most of our teachers were unmarried women (I found this very strange). In the last two years of my schooling some of them got married, but I still used to go to their houses.

In other words, I was accepted everywhere and felt comfortable everywhere but in my own home. At home I was surrounded by constant business troubles. I learned the word bankruptcy very early in life and whenever I came home from school to a grave atmosphere, I knew that my parents had just received another notice that one of their accounts in Warsaw had gone bankrupt. The financial anxieties and insecurities that I encountered at home still haunt me today.

To be fair, in addition to those Saturday walks, I can recall some positive aspects of my home life, like my father and mother reading the paper together every day and the whole family discussing politics or whatnot at the dinner table. Dinner was a time when everybody was together. After my mother took over the accounts in Warsaw, I remember her sitting down at the table with my father on Saturday night, after Sabbath, and working on the financial books.

I was never angry with my parents for not providing me with the life that my friends had. Somehow I sensed that it wasn't their fault. The one time that I really felt underprivileged was when there was a two-week school excursion to some historic cities of Poland. Because we just didn't have the money, this was a dream that I couldn't realize, and it was painful. All of my girlfriends went.

When I was in Grade 3 or 4, my sister's boyfriend gave me a pair of skates and I was in heaven because I could skate with all the other children. In the winter, instead of having gym inside, our gym teacher used to take us skating at a nearby park, on a pond that froze over for the whole winter. I don't remember the name of the park, but it had a few ponds and little islands that were connected with very charming bridges. We used the ponds for skating in the winter and for kayaking in the summer. For me, as a child, it was the most beautiful park in the whole world. It was superbly designed and had a few different levels. There were manicured lawns with the most colourful flowerbeds, wide pathways lined with old trees on both sides, and wide steps leading from one level to the next. The most romantic alcoves were hidden everywhere. There were benches in a circle under a canopy of tree branches that was so thick you could almost hide from the rain. At the very bottom were the few ponds with little islands connected by bridges. The areas around the ponds were open so one could roam around as free as a bird. The park, bordered by streets on all four sides, was enclosed by wrought-iron fences with gates that were locked at eleven o'clock at night.

In either Grade 4 or 5, I experienced something fairly traumatic at school. It was my turn – which was a privilege – to clean our teacher's desk. A big, blue heavy catalogue with all the pupils' names and addresses, along with the names of their parents and their occupations, sat on top. Beside my father's name was the word "worker." Well, I felt as though I could never live it down. I never mentioned it to anybody until now. In retrospect, it seems silly, but at the time it was a tragedy for me. I was terribly ashamed seeing my father called a worker; I wished that I could erase it. In the Jewish community at that time, being a carpenter, a tailor or a physical worker right away put you in a lower class; my parents had been educated and brought up in a business family. It was extremely important whether you came from a working – meaning uneducated – family or from a business family. This mentality stuck with me and affected my outlook on life for years to come. Outwardly, I wasn't an unhappy child, but I always knew I wasn't like the other children I went to school with and that I never would be.

I was a better-than-average student. Instead of letter or percentage grades we got "very good," "good," "satisfactory" or "unsatisfactory." If you had too many "unsatisfactory" grades you had to repeat the whole year. We got our grades twice a year – once before the winter vacation (which lasted two weeks) and then at the end of the year, before the two months of summer vacation. My grades throughout the seven years were mostly a combination of "very good" and "good" and if I ever got even one "satisfactory" in a subject, I was devastated. I was also not too bad in gymnastics, but I didn't swim and I didn't own a bicycle, so I could only ride one when a girlfriend allowed me to use hers. As a result, I never learned how to ride very well.

In Grades 6 and 7 the teacher recommended me as a tutor to some students who needed extra help, which the parents paid for. I was extremely good at tutoring and the students all showed great improvement in their grades, which made me feel good. I worked very hard with them; it was my first real challenge. It also gave me some extra money to go to the movies, which was the greatest pleasure available to me at the time. I continued this tutoring until the very end of school.

In my spare time after school I played softball with my friends. We also organized little plays amongst ourselves (in school I was quite often given parts in plays). I remember one role in particular – I was "Gapush," which in Polish means "silly little boy." I especially remember the part where I was looking all over for my galoshes because it was raining. In the play, I was late for school and I suddenly looked at my feet while repeating many times (in a very funny way), "Galoshes, galoshes, galoshes…." For the longest time all the kids in school kept calling out to me, "Gapush, where are your galoshes?" I guess I played my comical monologue very well.

Looking back on my school years, I can see that two aspects of my character really defined how I related to the world around me. One was my curiosity – my tremendous desire to experience and experiment, to try new places, to take chances and push ahead. Another was my need to be counted. I was always afraid to be unnoticed.

A New Path

When I was between ten and twelve years old, my mother used to put me on the train to Warsaw on some weekends, where friends of hers (the people she stayed with when she was there on business) picked me up at the train station. At other times I stayed with them for two weeks, but of course this was in the summer, during the school vacation. To me, it was a great adventure with new, strange people. They weren't religious Jews, but they were from a good family and they were quite interesting. They had four children much older than me: one daughter was a professional actress, which was considered a disgrace for any decent Jewish family; another daughter was very beautiful and involved with a married man (although at the time I didn't understand anything about it); a third daughter was physically disabled; and their son was simply no damn good.

Warsaw was a dream come true. After all, it's the capital city of Poland, with all the historical sites that I knew so much about from my history books. It's a beautiful big city (even by today's standards). The people I stayed with lived in a huge apartment building in a flat of six or seven rooms and the rooms were much bigger than the average rooms in Canada. That family gave me time and attention that felt unreal. They showed me all the interesting places, spending hours every day on something new.

On other occasions, my mother sent me to Zakopane, a mountain resort ten hours away by train, to stay with her sister-in-law and their children. They had moved there years before because one of her children had tuberculosis and their doctor had recommended the mountain climate. My aunt had a *pensjonat*, a small, very private, exclusive hotel. I had the time of my life there, with delicious food and lots of guests who kept taking me everywhere. But while I was there, I had my first problem because I was a girl. My cousin, a boy two years older than me, used to take me for walks in the mountains and my aunt, who was very religious, thought it was wrong. I had to leave earlier than expected. I couldn't understand what I had done wrong.

I often travelled alone to visit my relatives in Lodz, where my mother's two sisters, Manya and Sara, and my older cousins were very attentive to me. I also visited my father's sister, Baila, in the nearby small town of Sieradz. Her four children were very educated and already attended university. They too took good care of me. In addition to visiting relatives, I used any opportunity to be invited to my girlfriends' cottages. I would go anywhere to find a little piece of the nice life some other people seemed to have. I looked for a little sunshine wherever I could find it.

The economic depression in Poland was getting deeper and deeper and our family was feeling the effects, but continuing to scrape by. My sister married Herman, a very good-looking young man who was the son of the local owner of a barbershop and ladies' hairdresser. They were quite well off and even had a maid, but my parents initially viewed it as a tragedy – they thought that Fela was marrying beneath her because Herman was from an ordinary working family. The fact that my sister had a good life with them didn't matter. But their attitude slowly changed as their financial troubles increased. I guess they began to realize that being of a more refined background wasn't helping them to feed their family. I think that they also became a bit disenchanted with religion. My mother had changed a lot since she had started travelling for the business. She threw away her traditional Orthodox wigs and had her hair cut stylishly and set with curling irons. She became more sophisticated. She travelled by train in the company of businessmen. In other words, she was a pioneer, ahead of her time. Being in Warsaw so much, she slowly, a little at a time, began to question some of the more restrictive Orthodox Jewish religious traditions that would have prevented her from doing these things.

In Grade 7, when I was thirteen years old, my parents got an eviction notice from the landlord for not paying rent. We were forced to move to the other side of town, where, as I mentioned, there was a concentration of poorer working-class Jews and where the second Jewish school was located. I still continued to attend my old school, but I became part of a new world that we had more in common with economically, but less socially, because my parents were educated.

That same year – 1936 – was the beginning of three important years in my cultural, political and emotional development. I began to fall under the influence of some older students who belonged to Hashomer Hatzair, a Zionist organization that was very much to the left. I was ready to begin a period of questioning everything around me – up until then I had merely accepted things and just tried to get by. Now something different and new was happening to me. I began to think, analyze and search.

I joined the group and met girls whose brothers and sisters were members of an underground Communist group (being a Communist was illegal in Poland). I didn't even mention it to my parents – it was something one wouldn't dare to talk about. Some of them were in prison and I thought how shameful this must be for my new girlfriends because I didn't understand much about politics yet. Although there were many Zionist organizations with branches all over the world, Hashomer Hatzair had a reputation of attracting the most intellectual crop of Jewish youth. Apparently this was the case for the next fifty or sixty years to come, around the world and in Israel. (When I went to see Dr. Rakoff in 1972 after my husband's death, the minute I told him that I had been a member of Hashomer Hatzair, he wasn't surprised.

"I felt it," he said. He was originally from South Africa and had been a member of a group there himself.)

I had once again found a place where I tried to belong and fit in, a place where I could be accepted and fulfill the unsatisfied needs in my life. Those were my most positive three years, the years before I turned sixteen. My last year of school was just a question of passing time. In 1937, I finished with very high grades, but I was a very disappointed and bitter little fourteen-year-old. Most of my classmates went on to private high school in Lodz so they either lived there or commuted. The only high school in our town was very expensive and held classes on Saturdays, so only secular Jewish children could attend. Anyone who had the money went to Lodz.

I still remember how I felt in September when my friends put on their beautiful navy-blue uniforms with all kinds of insignias. The girls looked so cute in their boyish peaked caps. Did I ever envy them! I knew that our final separation was taking place. So I don't think it was a coincidence that I joined the Zionist group. Once again, it was a question of survival – replacing the old with the new – something I had to do so many times throughout my life. It almost became part of my existence. I was always waiting for another change and it became a normal way to live.

We moved again, this time to another smaller three-room flat. By that time one of my brothers, Yakov, had moved out, so we were only four children at home now. I was maturing emotionally and mentally very quickly, but I was still a fourteen-year-old girl without any future. I took some night courses and my parents sometimes found jobs for me at their relatives' factories for short periods.

Fortunately, I built a whole life within Hashomer Hatzair. There were children younger than me, members my age and others who were older. The organization consisted of small groups with a leader who was dedicated to instilling in us a love of Zionism with socialist ideals. We learned a lot about Marxism and Leninism, but the emphasis was on Zionism and the goal of collective living in kibbutzim in British Mandate Palestine. We were totally immersed in both Zionism and the idea of immigration to Palestine. The movement had a number of collective communes throughout Poland that were preparing to immigrate to pre-state Israel and experience the highest ideal of community living. We also had to participate in all kinds of sport activities and the emphasis on self-education was very strong. Our meeting place was in the library; there were a great number of quite capable kids like me who felt very cheated out of the opportunity for further education. Our reading assignments started with the basics: Alfred Adler's psychology and Sigmund Freud's psychoanalysis. We also had book-reading circles that involved first reading and discussing the books, and then writing papers on certain topics chosen by our leaders. I remember that I used to agonize over these political papers when it was my turn to write one. Fortunately, my older brother Fishel was very intellectual; he read an awful lot and was very well-informed politically, so he helped me. Actually, my whole family was politically well-informed, including both my parents.

The organization rented a small place in the centre of the city, which was convenient for everybody. It opened every evening at six o'clock as well as on weekends, and meetings were scheduled with a form of discipline as strict as in the army. We all mostly came from the same economic background, although a few of the members came from well-to-do families. Some were like me, from fallen heights, and some were from the lower working class. Of course, we were not all the same intellectually. But the emphasis on intellectual achievement was so great that everybody tried to do the best they could to improve themselves.

My parents, however, were very much against my membership in the organization. I was a non-believer and this was unacceptable, especially to my father. One time, I brought home a catechism written by a free thinker and read some excerpts from it to my father. I was lucky he didn't throw me out. Poor man, he knew he couldn't give me what I needed for my intellectual development. He couldn't send me to school. My mother kept quiet about it, though, and this made me feel closer to her. I empathized with her situation. Suddenly, I began to feel so very sorry for both of my parents. What a life – nothing from their children and so much struggle. I used to dream that if I ever got rich, I would see to it that they got a little bit of sunshine too. I also felt sorry for my little brother. I was quite protective of him and helped him with his schoolwork. He had a much harder time at home than I did because I was more resourceful in finding adventure and ways to travel. I was so much younger that I didn't feel very close to the rest of my brothers and sisters. They were nice enough to me, but I was building a world of my own, completely separate from them.

Another problem arose during this time. At a certain age, every Jewish girl was enrolled in so-called elementary Jewish religious studies, which was usually attached to a synagogue. I absolutely refused. "I don't need to learn how to pray," I used to say. "I'm not going to do it anyway." During certain Jewish holidays, such as Rosh Hashanah (the Jewish New Year) and Yom Kippur (the Day of Atonement), adults had to be in the synagogue from morning until sundown. Their children came to visit them sometime during the day. My parents, being Orthodox, were separated – women were upstairs in the balcony of the synagogue and men were on the main floor. I remember visiting my mother on those very holy days. The air was heavy and sticky and my mother, like all the women on Yom Kippur, was praying and crying very loudly. This was the day that they ask God's forgiveness for sins committed during the whole year. I was both appalled and scared by it. I couldn't understand why my mother would ask forgiveness for sins that, as far as I knew, she had never committed. I also couldn't fathom the whole idea of praying, addressing God and constantly praising him, using such powerful adjectives. Why? What for? I didn't dare to ask, so I would just fulfill my obligation to my mother, feeling sorry for her. Seeing her crying and humbling herself so much deeply touched me, but angered me at the same time.

For the most part, though, the Jewish holidays were a happy time in our family, a time of tradition and reunion that, to me, had nothing to do with religion. I used to love those holidays (except Yom Kippur, as I just mentioned). The transformation from an atmosphere of tension and worries over our constant financial problems was so great that it's no wonder that when I was happy I used to say, "I feel like it's a Jewish holiday today."

I especially felt this way on Passover. The house was cleaned in every corner and crevice, and it just had a different smell. Everyone got something new to wear – it was usually a new pair of black patent leather shoes. No matter how cold it was, I had to wear white knee socks with them. The routine of a holiday like this was so reassuring to me that it lifted my spirits. I used to dream about always having that kind of an atmosphere in my own house. The white tablecloth, the candles, the traditional seder (a dinner that follows certain rituals and tells the story of Passover, the ancient Israelites' exodus from Egypt), my father at the head of the table. I couldn't have cared less what they were reading in Hebrew, but seeing everyone so relaxed and cheerful meant a lot to me. I don't know how my parents managed to get all the customary food for the holiday, but it was there, and plenty of it. No one was allowed to talk business or politics (as we normally would). When I think about it, I am still amazed at how my parents (and of course other Jews of their generation) had the wisdom to use holidays in their survival kit.

There was an air of peace and tranquility in our house during the holidays and I just loved it. In the afternoons, whether we had visitors to our home or went out visiting, everybody was so polite, so cheerful. How did they manage to do it? What was the power that helped them transform so completely for just a few days? Did some people live in that holiday spirit all the time? When our holiday was over, the magic would be gone and everything went back to the old familiar situation.

When I later had my own family and we observed the traditional holidays, I must admit that I could never recapture that same feeling.

We went through the motions, but it was never the same as it had been when I was growing up. I was usually sad during those times. Even now, with my children and grandchildren around, I am still guilty of feeling sad, and I try desperately not to allow myself to turn back to the past. But as I said at the beginning, the little girl is very stubborn. She doesn't leave me alone.

~

Although I denied everything my parents stood for as far as religion went, I think that they came to appreciate me, perhaps even more than the rest of my siblings. They told me that I had the most feelings for them and, in general, that I was different. I had become a rebel as soon as I was capable of thinking about religion. But although I had no religious attachment, there was never a time when I wished I wasn't Jewish. I was born Jewish; I am neither ashamed nor particularly proud of it – it is just what I am. I accept everything that comes with it, except religion. Perhaps this sounds strange, but it's true. My special relationship with Judaism became evident during this time in my life and it is a relationship that stays with me today. It's my very own, unchanged throughout the years.

So, my two years after school were very exceptional in all areas of development. These were my years of fundamental change, the sort of changes that decide a person's future and leave a strong imprint on one's personality.

At Hashomer Hatzair, we had winter camps in our area and summer camps in the mountains, very much like the Boy Scouts here in North America. We stayed in tents and there was one building for activities such as cooking. We were trained in endurance; we went mountain climbing and on long, fifteen-kilometre hikes. It was a character-building place. Our camps turned out to be very memorable periods in my life. We met other young people from all over Poland who were socially and politically alert and spirited. There was a packed schedule of all kinds of lectures, meetings and study groups.

I recall some topics that we had to write essays on that were just un-believable. One in particular was "About Singing." For heaven's sake, how much can you say about singing? But when we heard some of the essays read out loud, I still remember my bewilderment – what one young man wrote about singing was just beautiful.

I always had a great admiration for spoken or written words, how one can use them in so many different ways, for so many different purposes: for good or evil, building or destroying. A combination of words can be used to describe feelings, another combination to make you laugh, make you cry, touch you at the bottom of your heart, comfort you or make you angry. Words hold a special magic for me and a beautiful speech is like music to my ears. My dream as a child was to never be short of words to describe or express whatever I felt and sensed at any given moment.

At Hashomer Hatzair, there was no competition – no grading and no praise – but the desire to be excellent was great in all of us. I don't think four years of high school could have given me so much general education.

I suppose our leaders, who were between eighteen and twenty, must have had some physical interaction between them, but this was not a dominant part of the experience. If there were any encounters, they were always discreet – to flirt openly, or even to wear makeup, was an unspoken taboo. As a matter of fact, I didn't even wear lipstick until God knows when. As for my sexual development, it progressed somewhat slowly. I got my period very late, I guess I was fourteen years old, and nobody had told me anything about it. My mother gave me a homemade belt with napkins. All she told me was that every girl at some age gets it. I adjusted to it fairly naturally, except that, of course, I didn't like the inconvenience of it. As for my bust, some girls my age were wearing some kind of brassieres, but I didn't need one until I was fifteen or sixteen years old. I don't remember exactly how I dealt with my sexual awakening. Nobody ever really explained inter-course to me. I remember knowing that in order to have a baby, a man had to be physically close to a woman, but when I heard how, I believe at twelve or thirteen years old, from some girls chatting the way they usually do, I was absolutely repulsed by it and didn't believe them.

How did I look at boys? Well, I liked them in a different way from girls. I liked to walk home with one boy who was the doctor's son and lived near me. I guess I learned instinctively to act differently with boys around, a skill I developed very early, now they call it flirting or being charming. In my early years of school, I wasn't the popular one among boys. Since there were so many pretty rich girls around, I didn't have much of a chance. Besides, we didn't have any pairing off in my environment until I finished school. So boys and sex weren't any part of my life yet, nor was it for my contemporaries, but we giggled about them. More than anything, I liked to dream about nice boys liking me, the ones I couldn't aspire to even come close to because of socio-economic differences. Again, this was a trait that stayed with me forever, dreaming the impossible dream, creating, in my fantasy world, the most beautiful situations and encounters. I just thrived on daydreaming.

The progression of my involvement with the opposite sex at Hashomer Hatzair was very nice, though. There was one boy who lived not far from me, so we used to walk in the evening together to our meeting room, our *izba*, and sometimes he would hold my hand while walking. But I remember one boy in particular, Hannanyo. I can still picture his face and I've kept his photo in my album. When I left home after the war broke out, we decided to correspond with each other. I had the most poetic letters from him, expressing his feelings for me in such an unusual way, so cautiously and delicately. He handled our friendship like something very fragile and exquisite, something pure and beautiful. I still regret not having his letters anymore. I can't remember why and how they got lost. He was very special to me, although we never even kissed. We were both sixteen years old. He had lost his mother when he was four years old and had huge, sad eyes. He always sat opposite me in the circle of chairs when we had our meetings or discussions and we would look straight into each other's eyes. This was just heavenly. When I came back after the war, I heard that he hadn't survived the Holocaust.

I also remember that at that point in time I allowed some of my friends to come to my place. I felt more comfortable with them, different from the way I felt with the wealthy kids I used to go to school with. I was more open, more myself.

One incident worth mentioning that I remember vividly was my father's unexpected visit to our camp. In the fall or winter of 1938, we had our camp about fifteen kilometres from town, which of course was walking distance for people of that era – even for a man of my father's age. This was the first time I had wanted to attend this particular camp and my father wouldn't let me go, saying, "What do you mean boys and girls together? And the food won't be kosher." He went on and on. I felt sorry for him, that he felt an obligation to oppose me, a young girl who he thought was heading down the wrong path. My mother was quiet again, not that she was so indifferent or lacking opinions – she was quite a woman – but she knew me and always believed in me. She was becoming more and more liberated from her religious upbringing and traditional values. On the second or third day of our camp in a rented house, one of the boys called out, "There's a man walking toward the house. Basia, it's your father!" I couldn't believe my own eyes – there was my father! He had walked all that way alone to see with his own eyes what his little fifteen-year-old girl was up to.

One of our leaders, a boy of nineteen or so, walked out to greet him and bring him in. There was silence in the big room where we had our meals and our meetings. It happened to be lunchtime and it was my turn to be in the kitchen. We had cooked a heavy vegetable soup with no meat, so they asked my father to join us, which he did. He kept looking around very politely, calmly and curiously. I don't remember how I reacted, but I am sure I was frustrated. The rest of the group was talking to him in Yiddish and Polish.

After lunch, they invited him to stay for our afternoon activities. The first was a great discussion, for which we all sat in an informal circle. I can't remember the topic, but everyone had to be prepared and would have already read about the subject. My father was very impressed with the seriousness of the group, with the intellectual level and with the amount of knowledge these young people had acquired. After that, I think we had some physical activities, whether tobogganing, if there was snow, or skating, I really don't remember. My father inspected our living quarters and saw that boys and girls were sleeping in separate rooms. He left much more assured about my innocence than when he arrived. I walked with him for a few minutes and he didn't exactly give me his blessing but he said that our leaders were very nice, responsible, idealistic young men. From then on I knew that my father understood me and I was thankful that he had come out to see it for himself. I knew that he now accepted me and whatever I stood for, even without his religion being part of my life.

~

One day when we came to the *izba*, we found that it was closed. Our leaders told us that the local authorities had locked us out because of our leftist activities. This was the biggest tragedy in my life up to then. I had lost a lifeline. I had lost the very essence of my existence. What followed was like a period of mourning. We would gather at different people's houses, undercover and at night, to continue with our meetings. After all, *aliyah* – immigration to Palestine – was our dream, a socialist Israel our ideal, and with it a new life in our land.

This closure went on for a few weeks and then our leader told us that this had been a test of our loyalties, of our stamina and perseverance. We had come through with flying colours. Our joy was unbelievable. We were all so ready to embrace something meaningful at the tender and very impressionable ages between thirteen and sixteen. If life didn't treat you well, you filled it with something. Fortunately, I had stumbled on a very positive, idealistic way of coping.

Taking Chances

I turned sixteen years old on June 10, 1939, although I never had a birthday party – I never celebrated my birthday in any way. That summer our organization held a two-month-long camp in the mountains that was twelve hours away by train from our town. One of my older brothers gave me some money and the rest was covered by the organization from donations they had received from wealthy supporters. The camp was again a great experience. The two months were just too short. I never wanted to go back home. Most of the people cried at our last evening party. The party wasn't something that North American teenagers would relate to at all. There was no alcohol – I don't think it even occurred to us to drink. There were no drugs, no smoking and no paired dancing, just the hora, a traditional Jewish folk dance. But we had so much fun; we sang Hebrew songs for hours, happy ones and sad ones. There was a lot of spirituality in the air, all with child-like innocence, and lots of laughter.

Two days before the end of the two months, at the end of August, we heard that negotiations between Germany and Poland had broken down. We knew this was the beginning. The danger of war was imminent. We had a hard time getting a train back home because the trains were being used for transporting Polish army soldiers. Our parents were worried about us and I felt a bit ashamed that I'd been off having fun. We arrived home and even before I reached my place, a friend of mine from school met me on the street and told me that my father was in the hospital with typhoid.

I'm not sure why, but my reaction to anybody being sick or having an accident, even someone's relative's death, had always been tremendous and out of proportion. For example, when my mother broke her leg when I was ten or eleven and they brought her home on a stretcher, I just couldn't deal with it. It was such a traumatic event for me. But I also remember that when my teacher announced my mother's accident in class, I was a big hero. For some reason I felt like one and my classmates treated me like one. I don't understand it at all. Another incident I remember from school was the death of the mother of one of my classmates. After that, I looked at him very differently. And when I was fifteen years old, my brother Fishel's wife died from an abortion done by a midwife. She had gotten some infection and died, leaving my brother with their little two-year-old daughter. Her death was something I absolutely couldn't handle; again, it's a reaction that I still have, to my great discomfort.

One thing that might have contributed to this extreme reaction was the fact that my father was a *cohen*, a priestly status in Jewish Orthodoxy. Being a *cohen* meant that he wasn't allowed near a dead body, to enter a cemetery or even be in a building after someone had died. When I was very little, a Polish neighbour of ours died and my father had to sleep at someone else's house until the dead man was buried, which took three days.

When I heard that my father was ill with typhoid I went to the hospital immediately. My father had lost a lot of weight and looked as if he was going to die. We couldn't get too close to him because typhoid is a very contagious disease and he was in quarantine.

When I returned home I also found out that my three brothers and my sister's husband had been called to the army and had already left. Luckily, a few days after I came back from camp, my father was well enough to come home. At this point, everybody was talking about the forthcoming war with the Germans. I really didn't know where to clue in first – my father being so sick, the war, my brothers going to fight for Poland…. the situation was, to me, quite unreal. I knew that big things were happening, but I didn't know where I fit in or how to process what was going on around me. I felt that nothing would ever be the same, but in my wildest dreams or nightmares, I couldn't imagine what would follow, that the first era of my life was coming to an abrupt end. Little did I know that almost everything around me, the familiar faces and places, would turn into memories – some to be cherished, some to be recalled with warm feelings, some with sadness and some with wanting to forget.

In our circle, most people were politically well-informed. We had known about Hitler coming to power and the problems Jews were having in Germany, so we knew that heavy clouds were hanging over all of us. But being so young, we couldn't sit and wait. Nobody could. Even people who had been through World War I didn't know what to expect. After all, Poland had been invaded numerous times by Germany or Russia, with some periods of peace in between. Everybody was waiting and talking about it. The Polish army had been mobilized to its full potential.

I must admit that I had a feeling of excitement deep inside me. I was waiting for something big to happen, something that would bring change, any change (little did I know how drastic the change would be). This feeling of waiting for a storm is powerful; it's all-encompassing.

As I have said, we had all begun to hear about the Nazi terror against Jews in Germany. As Polish Jews we were very much aware of antisemitism. We grew up hearing about it first in our homes, and then in school we learned about the persecution of Jews in Poland and all over the world through the centuries. I personally didn't question it – it was a fact of life that we were different and not accepted by other ethnic groups. But I had never really experienced antisemitism myself. The non-Jewish girls I played with before I entered school didn't consider me to be any different from them and my parents had some very good Polish friends. The only time I felt kind of awkward was during Easter parades, when I was told that no Jews dared to be on the streets. We were more or less warned to stay away. On the other hand, I didn't mind going to church sometimes with my non-Jewish girlfriends. As a matter of fact, I liked being there better than I liked being in the synagogue.

The preparations for war had been going on during the months I had been away at camp. The first sign of it was a bomb shelter dug up in our backyard, which happened to be an orchard a few miles long. We were living in the back of a small two-storey house, on the main floor. In the front were a food store and some living quarters. The landlords were Polish people who owned a large shoe store in the centre of the town. We never saw them around, except when it was time to collect the rent.

The next couple of days were full of anxiety. Poland was officially invaded on September 1, 1939. People gathered on the streets, waiting for news about the advance of the German army. The news on the radio was very hazy and unclear.

My friends from Hashomer Hatzair were in contact with each other a lot and our bond was even stronger. But I was also experiencing a new awareness of family. My sister lived with her in-laws, so with my brothers in the war and my father not well, I was now the oldest child in the house.

I remember the day when I woke up to the sound of warning sirens in full force: the air attack had started. The sound was deafening. My family and the people upstairs from us – an older woman with arthritis who was bedridden and her unmarried daughter – as well as the people from the front house rushed to the shelter.

The roar of the airplanes when they came down lower to unload their cargo was a sound that is impossible to forget. We all sat in silence against the wall of the very primitive shelter – it was almost what I would call a cave – except for my father, who kept up a steady stream of prayer, repeating over and over again, "Shema Yisrael," which means "Hear, O Israel." I have to admit that it really annoyed me. I didn't say anything to him, out of respect, but to me it was ineffective and almost ridiculous.

The bombing went on until dark that night. At that point, we went back into our house and saw the big holes that some of the bombs had made only two or three hundred yards away from us. We didn't scream at the sight of them or panic. It was as though we couldn't react yet. We behaved as if we were in a daze.

The bombing continued on and off for a few days. We could see fires in all directions, but none that were close to us. In the evenings my sister came over to check that we hadn't been hit and then went back to her place. On September 6, the Germans entered our town at the end furthest from where we lived. We were scared and didn't know what to expect. The Jewish people on our street were gathering to see what to do. They decided to flee to the countryside, even if only for the time being, to wait until the takeover had settled a bit. We packed a small wagon with our most necessary belongings and joined the long procession of Jewish families running away from the first onslaught of the German victors. What a sight. The city was burning in many places. It was already dark and my father was very weak; he was holding on to me while my mother and younger brother pushed the wagon.

There was a Polish farmer my parents had known for many years – he used to sell them poultry, eggs, potatoes and fruits for the winter. We headed toward his farm, hoping that he would let us stay with him until the air cleared and we could see what the Germans intended to do with the Jews in Poland. And he did. He gave us a place to sleep and fed us, doing it all without hesitation. We were there a few days, during which we experienced some tense moments. When the army passed by the farm we had to hide in the hay in the barn. Actually, we didn't even know at that point whether the Germans would hurt us. And I don't think they would have known who was Jewish unless the Poles told them. But we couldn't take any chances. After a few days, we decided that it was time to go back home and face the new reality. On the walk back, my father talked to me a lot, as if he knew that bad times were ahead of us. We found our house untouched, so we settled back to wait for what was to come.

Gloom and doom was in the air. People – I mean Jews – were still bewildered and Poles, well, I guess they didn't like it either but their lives were not under immediate threat unless they interfered with the new rulers. I remember the last Rosh Hashanah at home, when the melancholy mood had already settled over the house. The flickering candles seemed only to magnify our feelings. Fate had relentlessly intruded upon the life of our family. It felt as though it were almost laughing in our faces, saying, "You see – you complained before. What are you going to do now?"

∼

When we came home from the countryside, my parents' first concern was for their three sons in the army. Were they still alive? Had they been taken prisoner? Nobody knew anything. Then we began to deal with our daily survival, which meant adjusting to the very strict orders that were exclusively targeting Jews. The ordeal began slowly at first with a curfew – we had to be in our house by five o'clock in the afternoon. If we were caught on the streets after that, we could be arrested or shot. These rules were posted in public and announced on the radio. Later on, the Jews were all forced to live in a particular part of the city – which happened to be the neighbourhood in which we were then living – and that was the beginning of the ghetto in Zduńska Wola. I don't think that I can describe my reactions to all of this as a very idealistic sixteen-year-old. I was numb and the shock didn't wear off. I remember only too well my first encounter with German soldiers. There was a shortage of everything immediately and we needed bread. The father of a girlfriend of mine, Esther, had a bakery, so I decided to go and ask her if I could get some without waiting in the very long line-up. The bakery was located in the centre of town with

stores around it; in the middle was a big market square where merchandise could be displayed on portable tables. Nobody was in the
square when I went, as there was still so much chaos in the streets.
But as I walked over to the bakery, I saw a group of German soldiers
laughing very loudly, having real fun. As I got closer to the group, I
saw about eight or ten Orthodox Jewish men with long beards. The
Germans were forcing them to pull the hair out of each other's beards.
I could see the pain on their faces and hair flying all over; I heard the
Germans' laughter mixed with the faint, suppressed crying of the victims. I stood there for a few minutes, frozen to the spot. I couldn't
take another step. At that very moment, I knew that I wouldn't survive in Zduńska Wola. I ran home, forgetting all about the bread and,
crying hysterically, threw myself on my bed.

The days under the Germans passed without much thinking on
our parts. We couldn't afford the luxury; we had to preserve all our
strength to just get through each hour and each day. Meanwhile, two
of my brothers, Yakov and Abram, returned. It turned out that they
had been taken prisoner during the defence of Warsaw and then re-
leased. Fishel was still in prison. The battle in Poland had been over
in just under four weeks – it was just a breeze for the Germans. Now
life in our part of town was becoming somewhat normalized. People
were called back to work and food coupons were handed out as pay-
ment; it was enough to survive.

Then a new traumatic experience occurred – putting on the yellow armband that all Jews were required to wear by November 1939.
Somehow I determined it would only be temporary for me, although
I didn't have any specific plan – I really hadn't yet come to grips
with what was happening. I was lost in my own maze of anxieties
and wished that I could control my thoughts; strange and conflicting
emotions suddenly overpowered me. It's impossible for me to find the
words for what I felt.

My next experience was even worse. In the second week of
November, we heard that the Germans were rounding up all the

Jewish men. What could we do with my father? He wasn't well. He wouldn't survive. But where could he hide? The German soldiers came and dragged him out of the house to join the other Jewish men, pushed them into buses and drove to the Sieradz prison. Why? Nobody asked and nobody knew.

Fortunately, my father came back after two weeks, but what a sight. They had shaved off his long beard and he wore some ordinary old clothes and a cap. We didn't recognize him. My heart was breaking, along with my poor mother's. But at least he was alive. They had subjected the men to constant beatings and some hadn't survived. This was one of the first tactics the Germans used to scare us in preparation for what was to come.

At the same time, there was a great strength being born in me – a tremendous resistance and will to survive. We heard that our relatives in Lodz were starving. My mother's two sisters and their families couldn't even get any bread. I told my friend Esther, who was also a member of Hashomer Hatzair, and she gave me six two-kilogram round loaves of rye bread from her father's bakery. I put them into a big sack, threw it over my shoulders, took off my yellow band and walked to the railway station about twelve kilometres away.

I was determined to get on the train to Lodz – something indefinable was driving me. Whether I wanted to test my courage on top of wanting to help starving relatives I'm not sure, but either way, I had to do it. My parents didn't try to stop me from leaving and I boarded a train full of Germans. They even helped me up the few steps to the train. I did everything I could not to be noticed by some Poles on the train. I was at their mercy. I wasn't wearing my yellow band and all they had to do was point their fingers at me. I guess luck was with me. My relatives couldn't believe their eyes when I arrived. In retrospect, I can't say whether I did it for them or for a strange need in me to test my endurance under stress and fear. Was it all in preparation for the great moment to come?

One day, I saw my mother walking into the house looking completely discouraged and despondent. I knew right away what had happened because we had all been waiting for her. She had gone to get some bread and the line-up was very, very long. When five o'clock struck she had no choice but to come back empty-handed. The pain in her eyes was killing me. I picked myself up as if on command and quickly walked out the door. No one paid any attention to me. They probably thought that I was in one of my moods, that maybe I was going to walk around in a circle in the backyard as I usually did when the tension in me was unbearable. Again I took off my yellow band and I walked with my head up, with long steady strides, very deter- mined. I felt certain that if I just showed complete confidence, the Germans would not suspect that I was Jewish. I knocked on the back door of Esther's parents' bakery and when they opened the door, they looked at me in surprise. Not many words were exchanged. I only said that my mother had been here and had not made it to the front of the line. I didn't have any ration coupons with me, but they let me take a few kilograms of bread.

No weight would have been too heavy for me, but I must have ap- peared not very strong to one passerby. A tall German soldier behind me said in German, "Little girl, isn't it too heavy for you?" He was about ten steps away from me. I could almost hear my heart pound- ing with fear. My poor brain was racing like mad. What was I to say? I kept walking and didn't stop. There was no time to waste, though, and I had to come up with an answer for him. Suddenly, he was already beside me. "Please," he said. "Can I help you carry it?" I looked at him with my probably bewildered and fearful eyes and handed over my precious cargo. "Yes, it's heavy," he said. I still didn't know what to say. I already had a sense of impending disaster. The few minutes that had passed seemed a century long. "Where do you live?" he asked me. "Not far from here," I answered. "Please, I can carry it myself. It's not that far." By that time, some of my father's distant relatives from a nearby town had moved in with us as their town had pretty much burnt down. I felt that I was left with only one choice as we got closer to my house: to sacrifice myself in place of all of the people in the house.

As I have always done throughout my life, I thought through all the possible outcomes before deciding how to reach into the depths of someone's heart. My intuition was right, but luck was also with me again. I said gently, "You know that I am Jewish. As you can see, I took off my band. My mother came home without any bread and I can't stand seeing everyone go hungry tonight." He looked at me and said, "Okay, let's go to your house." "But we can't!" I responded. "Don't worry, I will not harm anybody." I didn't believe him and I was starting to feel desperate. "My father just came back from the prison," I said. "He won't survive seeing me walk into the house with a German soldier." "Please trust me," he said. "You can go ahead of me and tell them." I still didn't believe him but I went in anyway. I must have been shivering. "What is it?" Mother asked. "Are you cold?" "No, it's worse than that," I said. I told them the story and in walked the German soldier. There was dead silence. He spoke up first. "You have a very nice daughter; please don't be scared of me. I am just a man, like you. I also have a family and seeing this little girl carrying such a heavy load for her family, risking her life, touched something deep in me." Everybody took a breath of relief.

My father spoke perfect German. The man sat down at the table, asked for a cup of coffee if we had some and started a very normal, intelligent conversation with my father. Again, I don't have the words to describe the unreal scene. As the soldier was leaving, he emptied out everything he had in his military bag: sardines, canned meat, some chocolate. It turned out that he didn't approve of the whole damned war and, in a sense, he was also a victim.

Needless to say, we had a feast that evening and, better yet, the soldier showed up a couple more times for a talk with my father, bringing for us whatever he could. He was transferred out of Zduńska Wola before I left, and he came to say goodbye. Even if this man was only one isolated case, a drop of water in an ocean, it still reinforced in us the belief that there must be some decent human beings left among those Jew-haters, as we had initially perceived them all to be.

By November the weather had already grown colder and it became difficult to get coal. Winters in Poland can be very severe. Our places were heated by burning coal in big tiled ovens that were more or less like fireplaces. The heat from the ovens would radiate through the tiles. It was a very pleasant heat and we would sometimes leave the oven door open so we could look into the fire. I loved it. We used to throw in potatoes to bake on the burning coals. When the coal supplies suddenly dried up, I got a brilliant idea. The parents of Kazia Shapiro, one of my wealthy school friends, had a big textile factory. I remembered seeing a huge pile of coal in the backyard when I played at her place, which was just across from our orchard. Nobody would see me if I went in the dark, I thought. I made many trips, carrying the coal in big sacks, until I had accumulated enough for the whole winter. My girlfriend stood watch. I met up with Kazia after the war – she was one of the survivors I came across in Lodz. It's too bad I never saw her again after that. She was extremely bright and had enrolled at a university in Poland. As far as I know, she never left.

We had heard that the Soviet Union had signed a pact of neutrality with the Germans, known popularly as the Molotov-Ribbentrop pact. The Soviets took over the eastern part of Poland, next to their border. Then we heard rumours that there were Polish Jews who were escaping to the Soviet-occupied area. Some of my friends' older sisters or brothers were intending to leave. Of course, everything was being organized in great secrecy. When I heard about it, I didn't even dare to think about it for myself at first. Then I tried to talk my parents and my whole family into leaving – we really had nothing to lose. But to my father, the Soviet Union was a godless society, so it was unthinkable for him. Besides, it wasn't easy to get to the border. We would have to travel by train to Lodz, then to Warsaw and then to the small town of Małkinia, where there was a strip of land that was on the border between the German and Soviet-occupied areas. One could get caught at any moment. We never talked about my suggestion again – it had been instantly dismissed.

But the idea of leaving home was in my head, drilling and drilling its way through, and I continued to get more and more depressed and increasingly restless. I just didn't know where to begin. I didn't have any money, not even enough to buy the first train ticket. So as much as I heard about some young people's plans, I couldn't really crystallize my thoughts at all. How and with whom could I go? Then I started to verbalize my thoughts. My father just shut me up, but my mother, as always, was listening. As time went on, I became obsessed with the idea. The more we felt the Germans' heavy boots in our lives, the more I knew that I had to leave. All my instincts were telling me to go, but I was scared. Where was I going to go and what would I live on? I had no occupation and would be all alone.

I used to lie in bed at night, giving in to my fears about leaving. And then I tried to tell myself that each one of us must find our own way, even though the entire world might be set on fire, even though everything might be in turmoil; each one of us had to take on the final responsibility for action. The idea of leaving persisted and completely consumed me. I couldn't think of anything else. My parents worried that I was losing my mind. I would go out during the day, meet with my friends, come home – leaving was all I could talk about. My siblings were content to stay and wait. They hoped for better times, but I couldn't see that in the future.

My parents argued about me all the time. Meanwhile, I was working at full speed, trying desperately to attach myself to a group of young people older than me who were planning to escape. I contacted some of them through my Zionist organization and finally persuaded them to let me join one particular group. But I needed two things: my parents' permission and some money – first to pay for the train and then, if we made it to the border, for a smuggler, a Polish farmer living in the area who knew how to get people across.

My campaign to leave had taken a couple of months and finally, near the end of December 1939, my parents said to each other, and to me, that they had no right, in a time of war like this, to hold me back. Maybe this was my fate. It required all my strength to hold back my tears. The tension of the last weeks was now overshadowed by the thought of parting, the final break and the total uncertainty of the future. My parents couldn't give me any money, though. My sister and one of my brothers gave me a little and the group took me in with less than the required funds.

I remember the last night I spent at home. I was very scared. My mother asked me what I was going to do to support myself in a strange place, with no skills. I said, "I will wash floors and not take anything from the Germans." I packed a knapsack and said goodbye to my family. Only my mother took me to the bus station where I was to meet the group to go to Lodz, our first leg of the trip. I wasn't wearing the yellow band because Jews weren't allowed to travel from town to town. We walked and talked; this was the last time I saw her. I had to detach myself quickly from any feeling of loss or sorrow. I needed every bit of strength to get to my destination, to be free.

Entering a New World

When I got to the bus station, my group was already there. There were two girls from the Zionist group who were older than me. Adela, a tough, sturdy, down-to-earth, very plain girl from a working-class background, was honest and good-natured. She gave me a sense of physical security, but intellectually we had nothing in common. Lonia, the older sister of my very good friend Sara, was also from a working-class background, but she was intelligent, shrewd and very left-wing. She was also quite attractive. There were three young men I didn't know very well. Two of them were from the Sztainhorn family, Henry and Abraham, who were older brothers of my school girlfriend Bela, one of the girls who went to private school. They came from a well-to-do, very religious home. They were fine boys, clever young men with a lot of integrity, but because of their religious upbringing and restrictions, they had a difficult time fitting in with us. The third boy was Srulek Lipman, who was also from our Zionist group and older than me. I had never had much of an impression of him; he was nice-looking and clean cut, from a religious family. His mother had died when he was two years old. There were six of us in total.

Everything had been worked out beforehand. We had to act as if we were strangers but follow each other and not get lost. None of us wore our yellow bands, of course, and we arrived in Lodz safely. From there, we took a train to Warsaw, again arriving safely. We had to stay there for a few days until we could find a contact to a smuggler. Somebody knew a Jewish woman who let us stay with her, for pay, and she also helped us get in touch with other people who had the same plans. We were successful in finding the contact, a Polish farmer, and everything was arranged. Now came the worst part of the trip – boarding a train in Warsaw that would take us to the border town of Małkinia. There were Germans all over the place. We had to hide from the Poles, who would identify us as Jews, and avoid the Germans because we didn't have the necessary travel papers. We only had to go a short distance to the train station, but we still had to board the train and nothing was running on schedule. It had only been a few months since the Germans took over and everything was still in chaos. We were running like crazy from one ramp to the next, under bridges, on top of rail tracks – nobody knew which train went where. I really panicked. At one point, I found myself on the track down below the platform with a train coming toward me. I was sure that this was the end of me. I couldn't pull myself up, but at the last second Henry Sztainhorn pulled me up and literally saved my life.

Fortunately, the group safely arrived at the spot designated by our Polish farmer on the edge of a forest. It was already dark and all he said to us was, "Just follow me, but keep a distance from each other. If they shoot, lie down." He described the spot where we would meet once across the German-Soviet frontier and told us that while we crossed we were on our own and that it was our responsibility to watch out for German border guards. The width of this "no-man's-land" was about three kilometres. I don't know what I was thinking. My adrenalin kept me going. Any fear, if it was in me, was suppressed. My animal instincts alone were directing me, pushing me ahead. Then I heard shots. I lay down as I had been told and the shooting stopped. I was trying not to lose sight of my companions. We were shot at three separate times. I guess the Germans heard some noises but couldn't see us in the dark forest. I don't know how long it took to cross this piece of land, but it felt like an eternity. We all arrived safely at the described spot and waited, huddled up until morning. We were now on territory that was occupied by the Soviet army. Early the next morning, we walked over to the quarters of the local Soviet authorities and turned ourselves in. It was December 1939.

From this moment on, we became part of the new breed of *biezhenietz*, which in Russian means "refugees." By now, the Soviets were used to people like us running from the Germans, but they still put us through a lot of silly questioning. Our interrogators in this case were Ukrainians, but our guide, who lived in this part of Poland, understood Ukrainian and served as a translator. After a few hours, the Soviet soldiers drove us to the nearby city of Bialystok, where most of the *biezhenietz* stayed when they first arrived. We were taken to a big synagogue full of people like us, just a drop among the millions of Polish Jews who didn't leave. The six of us from Zduńska Wola stayed together. We had been thrown together for better or worse. There was no special personal involvement between us, just a common will to survive.

The noise and the stale air in the synagogue were stifling. I was completely disoriented. Some authorities dealt with us again, but this time they were local Jewish people. The *biezhenietz* were all different ages, mostly young, but I think I was the youngest. The authorities tried to absorb us into different, smaller communities, towns or villages around Bialystok. For our group, they picked a village by the name of Kuźnica, about fifty kilometres away. After a few days we were taken to this typical small Polish town of two or three thousand people, mainly farmers who supported the mostly Jewish local tradesmen and storeowners. Again, the local authorities took us to the synagogue, a much smaller building. It was just one large, plain room with a big tile oven in the middle of the wall that was similar to the one we had at home.

Standing at the tile wall was a young boy about my age with his hands behind him, warming himself against the wall. He was a very good-looking boy of medium height, with dark, penetrating eyes and very fine, chiselled features. He was dressed in a nice suit, which surprised me, and he looked quite different from the rest. He seemed reserved, quiet, rather serious looking, kind of sad and kind of introverted, yet with a pride that was very obvious within him. I caught his glance instantly and he caught mine. His name was David Recht and eight years later, he would become my husband. But it didn't happen just like that. Years went by before we even knew that we liked each other or that there was anything going on between us. All those years, everybody else seemed to think that we liked each other, although sometimes we were not even living in the same place. I used to say that if worse came to worst, I could always marry David.

David had escaped from Lodz with his younger brother, Isaac, an adorable little boy of twelve. Being so very young, David had managed to get him into an orphanage home in Bialystok and they were able to visit each other once a week. David had left behind his mother and an older sister. For the most part, it was the Jewish men who felt insecure – many people didn't think the Germans would treat women as badly. What a naïve hope!

In those first few days at the synagogue, I met other young people from Lodz and from my hometown. I don't know how they had gotten here and whether it was a coincidence that they were in Kuźnica. There was one other girl, Bluma Chabelak. She was eighteen years old and had escaped with her older brother. I had only known her vaguely back home because she travelled in different circles. She came from an extremely well-to-do family, but was very plain. She grew up in luxury and blossomed into a beautiful, gentle flower. She had blond hair, big blue eyes, very fine features and a nice smile, showing beautiful, even teeth. Her clothes were expensive and in good taste. She was one of those lucky ones back home who attended the local high school, which put her in a different category right away. She was very reserved, even shy, but articulate, intelligent, sweet and soft-spoken.

There were also three more boys from our hometown. Aaron Liebowicz, a tall blond boy with blue eyes, who was eighteen years old and looked like a typical Polish young man. I hadn't known him in Zduńska Wola; he was of average intelligence and was very witty, with a beautiful singing voice. Then there was Shashewsky, who I remembered from school. He was two years older than me and was nice, polite and fairly intelligent. The last one, Meyer, I didn't know at all. He was nineteen or twenty years old and had worked in a bank. He was dressed immaculately and kept company with Shashewsky. I was told that he was a "bird" – in Yiddish that meant a gay man. I really didn't understand what that entailed except that they liked boys rather than girls. I never went beyond this knowledge. I simply didn't pay attention to it and nobody talked about these things until I came to Canada. I was in my mid-forties before I understood what homosexuality meant in a physical sense.

In the synagogue in Kuźnica, the Jewish townspeople built some bunk beds for us and brought some bedding and food. I still couldn't think straight. Sure, I was free and my life wasn't being threatened, but the drastic, sudden change was taking its toll on me. I still couldn't believe that I was there; it was like a dream. All my energies were directed into holding myself together. I had this Humpty Dumpty feeling that if I ever allowed myself to break down, no one could ever put me together again.

After being there for a couple months, some Jewish families from town came to the synagogue and looked us over. One couple approached me and asked how old I was. When I answered, they asked me if I would like to live with them. I was delighted. The man was the local tailor; he and his wife had a few children of their own and lived in a nice little house. They even gave me a room to myself, which was a luxury, and I felt like I was part of the family. They had very different customs from the Jews I had known at home. Being tailors, they were also people from a different class than my family. Nonetheless, I was very thankful for their hospitality and considered myself lucky.

I was still very much part of the *biezhenietz* group in the synagogue, which was where I really felt I belonged. Most of them found some kind of work – the Soviets made sure everybody worked even if it meant carrying barrels of big stones from one place to another for a whole day. I wasn't sure what I was equipped to do, but one of the local Jewish boys knew people at the railway station in Bialystok and said that he might be able to get me a better job than manual labour. So he took me to the Bialystok station office and to my great joy I wound up with a job as a conductor on a sleeper – a Soviet train that went on twelve-hour trips to various places. Senior army officials travelled in those sleepers and I was to be responsible for their well-being, serving them tea, giving them towels and so on as well as collecting their tickets. The pay was really minimal, but I accepted it.

I had to find a place to live in Bialystok during the week, but I continued to come back to Kuźnica for my days off, whenever they happened to be. Living spaces were very limited because most families had to give up rooms for the men who were serving in the army. I wound up staying with a very attractive Polish lady who was probably in her forties. She had three bedrooms: one for me, one for her and one was for a very handsome Soviet officer who also happened to be her lover, as I could often hear at night. This was my first exposure to many things, including smoking, the first sign of women's liberation. In my hometown, it was unthinkable for a woman to smoke, but even if she did, walking around on the street smoking was something else entirely. I still couldn't do it.

My job was another overwhelming experience. Bialystok is a very big railway hub that connects many cities. It was terrifying to even find the train I was supposed to work on. And how would I communicate with the Soviets? The office people were Polish so at least I could understand their instructions. On my first assignment I was to be away for three days, home for two days, and so on. I finally found the train and the car I was assigned to. I had to be there several hours early to make sure that the samovar (Russian tea urn) was in good working order and see to the linens and so on. As I was waiting for the Soviet officers to arrive, loneliness started to set in. I stood near the window, trains all around me, in the middle of the special hustle and bustle of a very busy railway centre. It was dark and I could see the stars in the sky. Where am I? I thought to myself. Who am I? To whom do I belong? It was the first time that I had felt this way since I had left home. The feeling had been with me from a very young age, but now it surfaced with tremendous power. Suddenly I was gripped by fear. Where was life leading me? I felt like a lost child, a little girl wandering around in a big world.

I just stood there, tears pouring down my face, feeling so lost and desolate, waiting for my superiors, scared to death. The first one to arrive noticed my tears. He said something in Russian that I didn't understand. He smiled faintly and touched my head, like a father. Then the others arrived; some were high army dignitaries and luckily they were all very proper. My job was to serve them tea and open the door at stations and see if anybody was coming on or getting off. The rest of the night I could even doze off. The first few nights I had to pinch myself to feel that it was me. It was all so unreal.

I lasted about four weeks in this job until fate turned things around again. On one trip, I closed a very heavy door on my finger. Well, they rushed me to the hospital and had to remove my nail because of the danger of gangrene. It was done without any anesthetic. It may have been available to the military, but not to civilians. I even had a tooth extracted a few years later without any freezing. I was glad that this was the end of my new career. I went back to the tailor's family in Kuźnica for good. It was now my home.

At this point, I started the first real romantic involvement of my young life. There was a local general store owned by a very nice and respected religious Jewish family who had three daughters and one son. Everybody in town knew the *biezhenietz* – to them we were a local attraction, something new in their dull lives. They didn't have German occupiers and although it was true that the Soviets put many restrictions on them, their lives were still relatively untouched by the war. Their son, Chaim, who was about twenty-three, had been fighting with the Polish army in the war and came back with his wounded arm in a sling, obviously very proud of it. That made him different in my eyes right away. He came around regularly to the synagogue, like most of the local young Jewish people. I kind of liked him, but I wasn't very experienced. I knew how to chat and smile, but he knew much more than I did and he went after me. He invited me to his parents' house and they treated me with kindness – after all, I was a girl of sixteen and a half, all alone, and they had an eighteen-year-old daughter. But my new friend had more than kindness in mind and slowly made his move. He was the first man I was intimate with, an experience that was new and strange to me. It happened without any warning or any talk, very naturally. I remember that afterward I looked for signs of blood. I felt kind of wet, but to my great surprise, there was no blood. I was very disturbed and worried. Could I have already lost my virginity without a man? I wouldn't talk to anybody about it.

At that time, nobody talked about sexual experiences. You weren't supposed to do it. You could kiss and hug and pet, but not that. I lived with the secret a long time until I found out that women don't always bleed. A girl can lose her virginity under all kinds of circumstances, such as playing sports, without ever knowing it. I got very attached to this young man – being seven years older and very experienced, he became everything to me. The warmth of his family and the feeling that I belonged to him sustained me. Did I love him? I didn't really know then what love was. If what I felt can be called love, then I was in love; really, though, my circumstances created my very strong dependence on him.

I began to miss my parents and my family. Sometimes I got so desperately depressed and lonely that I allowed myself the luxury of feeling sorry for myself and would cry quietly in bed in my room. Not long after Chaim and I got involved, I received the following postcard from my mother:

May 11, 1940, Zduńska Wola

Dearest Basia,

I have written you a few letters and haven't received any answer. I don't know what to think anymore. My sleepless nights, the tears that are pouring out of me, you can't imagine. My dearest Basia, I beg you, write me a few words. How are you? Do you at least have something to eat? Are you healthy? Dear Basia, maybe it will be possible for you to obtain a permit and come home. It is my greatest desire to see you. Maybe you don't have money for the journey, in which case I will send you money; just do your best to get the permit. Thank God, everything is all right with us; we are all healthy. Fishel came back from captivity and he feels well.

Regards from everyone,

Your loving mother.

～

Summertime was approaching. My romance with Chaim was in full bloom. David was around, as well as other boys from the groups that had escaped Poland, but I was privileged, keeping company with a local boy. I knew that quite a few of the local boys liked me. I think my group knew about my involvement and they didn't approve of a young girl like me having an intimate relationship. I was being very discreet but I didn't care what they thought. I felt that I was fortunate in finding something to sustain me, something to help me make my life bearable.

∼

July 12, 1940, Zduńska Wola

Dearest Basia,

We were all very delighted to receive a letter from you. We all thank you for writing. You write that I don't write very much. I have the same complaint against you. The amount of joy my writing evokes in you cannot compare to our joy. There hasn't been a day that I haven't talked about you, there hasn't been a meal where I haven't said, Basia certainly doesn't have this food. There hasn't been a Saturday that you haven't been mentioned. I very much regret that I let you go, but I hope we'll see each other soon. Thank God everything is fine with us, we are healthy. Thank God we don't lack anything – one can get everything for money here. In general, it is quiet in Zduńska Wola, but in Lodz our brothers and sisters suffer from hunger. Dear Basia, you write that I should send you 20 marks, but it is too difficult for us. Why didn't you write your address? I would have tried to send you as much as possible. You asked how we are making a living. Until the ghetto was closed, I used to go to Lodz and I was able to earn a fair amount of money, but it is no longer possible to go. We only earn a little here, but, thank God, we are making a living. Fishel and Abram work little but earn a few zlotys for themselves. Yacov married Łajka a few months ago. I will send you a letter so everyone has room to write.

From me, your loving mother, who wants to see you as soon as possible.

∼

Since receiving these two postcards, some questions tormented me. Was what I did intolerable? Had I done it out of a selfish, childish wish for adventure? I couldn't help but realize how much pain I had caused them, especially my mother. I never knew how much she loved me. She had almost all of her other children around her, yet she worried about me. Why hadn't I been able to see it while I was at home? Why hadn't she been able to put it into words then, as she did now? I know she wasn't trying to make me feel guilty; I fully believed her anguish.

When my oldest brother, Motek, immigrated to British Mandate Palestine, she talked about him all the time, wrote to him and sent him parcels. It makes me think, how can one mother have enough feelings and concern for seven children yet, in the world I live in today, seven children sometimes can't take care of one mother, sending her away instead to a nursing home? This thought makes me particularly sad.

I was torn apart after reading these postcards. My mother was asking me to come home and I had asked her to send me twenty marks for the journey. Coincidentally, almost as if the script for my life had been written a long time ago, the local Soviet authorities made a public announcement at almost this same time that if any of the refugees wanted to go back to German-occupied Poland, they would provide transportation. There were posters everywhere. All we had to do was register, so I did. What perfect timing, I thought – I would be back with my family and share their fate no matter what. But it turned out that the scriptwriter was laughing at me. This wasn't at all what the Soviets intended – that would have been much too simple.

There were rumours that something bad was going to happen to us, but we still wanted to believe that they would send us back. We felt misplaced; we felt lonely; we felt homesick; we had begun to forget why we had left home in the first place. We forgot what the Nazis stood for – time and distance can accomplish a lot. It was already near the end of the summer of 1940. My boyfriend's brother-in-law had information from the Soviets and he warned us what was coming, told us that the Soviets would try to talk us into going deep into the Soviet Union, but we didn't believe him.

I remember that David's younger brother was visiting him at the time and begged David to join him if they forced us to go somewhere. But David felt that it wasn't fair to take his little brother out of a secure, comfortable environment and drag him into the unknown. Tragically, only one year later, when Germany declared war on the Soviet Union and marched into Bialystok, little Isaac was lost forever. Nobody even knew when or how. David couldn't forgive himself.

One night, I was asleep in my room in Kuźnica when I heard a knock on the front door and somebody answered it. Suddenly, my door banged open and I heard loud voices shouting. I must be having a nightmare, I thought. I saw two Soviet soldiers pointing their rifles at me with the bayonets out. I was speechless. They were shouting at me in Russian, but I was in such a state that it could have been Polish and I still wouldn't have understood them. They motioned to me to get dressed. They wouldn't move and stood there watching me while I took off my nightgown and got into my clothes. They allowed me to pack up my few meagre possessions. I followed them and waved goodbye to my bewildered family in the window, feeling like a criminal. What crime had I committed? It took me years of living in the Soviet Union to realize that this country was full of criminals like me – criminals who hadn't committed any crime.

I followed the soldiers to a truck that was already filled with other refugees from Poland in the town. We looked at each other in disbelief. They had tricked us. Anyone who had said that they wanted to go back home to Poland was now considered an enemy of the Communist state; as people from a capitalist country, we couldn't be trusted. We were to be interned and were now heading to a labour camp in the far north, in Arkhangelsk, further north than Siberia.

I began to sob hysterically. Although losing my boyfriend was not the same as losing my whole family, at the time all I felt was another heart-wrenching loss. Another parting; another change. This was what my life would be like for a long, long time. We travelled a few hours on the truck until we reached the train station in Bialystok, where we were joined by many others who had been similarly rounded up.

Arkhangelsk Labour Camp

We were put onto big, covered train cars that were used for transporting cattle, thirty or forty people to a car. Throughout the journey, we were given food and slept on straw mattresses. At certain stops in the middle of nowhere we were allowed to get off the train to attend to our physical needs in the open fields. We were warned from the beginning not to try to escape, that we would be shot instantly if we did. I heard that some people from other cars tried, but I don't know what happened. The trip lasted four weeks. You can only imagine the conditions, the dirt and stink. I wasn't really alone, but I missed my new and very first boyfriend terribly. In a way, our relationship was still a blessing because at least I had some nice memories to fill my mind and push out what was happening in the present.

We finally arrived at our first destination, a big city in the state of Arkhangelsk. We were unloaded from the train and put into huge trucks driven by guards, as if we were prisoners, through thick forests for hours and hours until we arrived in a big, open area with rows of low buildings – the barracks we would be living in. We got off the trucks and were told to gather in one place. There were about two or three hundred of us in all, along with the local authorities who were our guards. A high-ranking officer gave a speech that was translated into Polish. In it he told us that we were in the midst of a lumber-producing region, surrounded by thousands of miles of impenetrable forest. We would be working in the forest, cutting down trees to be shipped down the river. We would be assigned sleeping places in the barracks and there was a big kitchen with an eating hall and other facilities. In the middle of the area were the houses for the guards. The officer told us that if anybody ever attempted to escape, they would be tracked down and shot. This was our welcoming speech.

We were divided into different camps at random. I looked frantically for my friends from Kuźnica – David, the two Sztainhorn brothers, Aaron Leibowicz, Adela and Bluma. I tried to stay with the two girls, especially Bluma. There were very few girls, or women I should say, in proportion to men. They gave us a separate barracks, where I met other girls from many cities in Poland, some with whom I became very friendly and formed close relationships. We had to depend on each other for moral and physical support.

The barracks were huge empty rooms with rows of narrow iron beds; two rows of beds stood two feet apart and each two-row set was separated by four feet. The men's barracks had about forty beds – in other words, forty men in one room. We women had smaller barracks and we had some shelves and some hangers on the walls for our possessions. Next they took us to the dining hall, which had rows of long wooden tables and chairs. The kitchen staff were all Russians and the waitresses were very wholesome, sweet-looking Russian girls.

The next day, the guards picked us up in trucks to take us to the places where we would be cutting down trees, men and women alike. It was still fairly warm, so we didn't know what to expect in the winter. Even so, although it was September, there was ice around the water well where we got our water. Every group was accompanied by a couple of guards who showed them how to cut down the huge trees with handsaws. The men were given all the saws; we girls were given axes and shown how to chop all the branches from the fallen trees. I had never held an axe in my life.

We weren't paid for the work, only given coupons that we could exchange for food and not much more. The men had a quota system, with rewards for the biggest production. Every group elected a leader. For the first couple of weeks, we didn't take our situation seriously. It felt like a camp, so we laughed and joked, but slowly our good spirits disappeared.

In the beginning, I shared a bed with my girlfriend Bluma. A few of us had to do this since there was a shortage of beds. But then Bluma got sick with tuberculosis and was taken to a small hospital nearby. I began to run a steady, higher-than-normal temperature too, so I guess the authorities were afraid that the illness could spread and they took me off the forest work. I was lucky to be given the job of washing the floors in the barracks. Four or five of them were under my jurisdiction. The floors were made of wooden boards that I had to wash every day. It was a really gymnastic feat to manoeuvre my way between and under those heavy iron beds.

Despite the difficulties, what I was doing was actually privileged work and all the other girls envied me. Didn't I say before deciding to leave home, "I will wash floors. I will do anything." What a self-fulfilled prophecy! I didn't think about the fact that I could also have gotten seriously ill, that thanks to Bluma I had been saved from doing the heavier work. David also got very sick and they took him to the hospital where Bluma was. I used to visit them both occasionally.

There were a few other girls who also had what was considered to be privileged work. Two of them worked in the steam bath where men and women could sometimes go to get clean. People kept more or less clean and they inspected us regularly. A few girls worked in the laundry room, which meant washing big, rough sheets by very primitive means. Another girl, Lola, from Warsaw, got a job working in the bakery, which was even better. Lola used to smuggle big chunks of delicious crusty white bread baked for the Russian guards and other staff out of the bakery and give them to me when we met at the water well to fill up the two big pails of water we had to carry in each hand. She needed water for the bakery and I needed it to wash the floors.

I was often tempted to eat the bread myself, but decided against it because the guilt of not sharing it with some of my friends would have overpowered the pleasure of eating it. Lola couldn't take any bread when she left work for the day because she was searched, so she really trusted me. I never even stole one single bite for myself.

Lola was much older than the rest of us. She was married and I think she had a child somewhere. She was like a young mother to us and was very good-natured and easy to be with. Ala, also from Warsaw, was in her late twenties and not married; she wasn't very pretty but she was tall and slender with beautiful clothes. I don't know how she had been able to carry them all with her across the border. She was a manicurist or hairdresser in Warsaw and was immaculately clean; she was a very nice person and easy to be with as well.

Another girl I met was Feiga, a little blond girl from Wilno who was unlike anyone I knew. She belonged to a movement of social-ist Jews called the Bund that advocated the cultural autonomy of Jews within the countries they lived in, rather than immigration to Palestine. They were very much against Zionism and were very Jewish without practising religion – so-called secular Jews. They improved the Jewish language (Yiddish) from jargon to a regular language with grammar, a proper dictionary and so on. They also had their own schools, where Polish was taught as a second language and everything else was in Yiddish. They revived Jewish culture and literature, and believed in a socialist society. This movement was le-gal in Poland before the war, where there were many other socialist Polish organizations.

Wilno was known as the cradle of Jewish culture. Feiga's father was principal of a leftist high school where the subjects were taught entirely in Yiddish; her mother was a teacher there and Feiga was a graduate. She was only eighteen years old when I met her, so maybe they started their school earlier than we did. Feiga was brought up so differently from us – we never spoke Yiddish amongst ourselves, though I understood some, I had only spoken Polish with my parents and siblings. Feiga spoke a totally different language that was very cultural, using expressions we had never heard. She called it literary Yiddish. She was short, only five feet (I was 5 foot 2 inches), and was a very direct, honest, solid girl; I didn't quite get her and she remained a mystery to me. Still, out of the whole group, we were the only two who sat down every evening, right from the beginning, to work at learning Russian from the newspapers that we asked the guards to give us. By the end of our time in the camp we could communicate quite well in Russian, something that would soon serve us both very well.

There were two sisters from Kalisz, a bigger town than Zduńska Wola and not far from it. The older one, Lola, was also unmarried and was very skinny with a long nose and dark, curly hair. She was a very disciplined, hard worker and reliable, very fair in her judgments. Her sister, Hela, although not very pretty, was pleasant, cheerful, articulate and quite intelligent. She was one year older than me. I noticed that a lot of brothers and sisters had escaped together. Two other Polish sisters lived in our barracks as well – they were the daughters of a high Polish officer from Wilno. Wanda, the elder one, was just gorgeous, like a Polish princess, with very light blond hair, deep-set blue eyes, tall, slender, beautiful legs and a majestic walk. Any man would fall in love with her. Her younger sister was just the opposite, not much to look at but a nice girl, no trouble to anybody.

There were also some married couples I didn't know as well who had small rooms to themselves. A lot of the boys our age or older used to visit our barracks during our weekly day off in the summer, but not usually in the winter. When spring came, we used to meet them on the edge of the forest for little walks, talks or just socializing. David was among them and paid a lot of attention to Wanda. I often saw them walking together, but that's all. He also paid attention to me. It's funny that Wanda used to say to me, "Basia, I think David likes you." It didn't bother me one way or another – after all, I had experience with a much older boy and he was still in my thoughts, when I wasn't too tired to think. Everybody liked David – I think it was because he was so good-looking – but I didn't feel anything for him then. Maybe he was too young for me. One thing that I did like about him a lot was the fact that he was completely unaware of his good looks; he couldn't have cared less. He did try to impress people, but only with his knowledge. He read an awful lot and was always talking about astronomy and science fiction, subjects of no interest to me. He was a shy boy with a lot of stamina – he was very strong, determined and disciplined, and was at the top of his work team. I thought that he was too serious, too heavy-minded for me. Chaim, the boy from Kuźnica, was more fun to be with.

As far as we knew, none of the girls – except Feiga – was involved with anybody. I don't think we cared. We weren't very well physically – we had all stopped having our periods and most of us, including me, were constantly suffering from big boils under our arms or on our legs. I have such huge scars from them that some people later thought I had had surgery done in those spots.

As for Feiga, she was involved with a nice man from Warsaw who was a fellow member of the Bund and a teacher in their schools, a rather handsome man. They had a lot in common. He had been married before the war, but I don't know what happened to his wife. He was at least fifteen or more years older than Feiga. We knew for sure that she was intimate with him, but we didn't condemn her for it – we just felt strange about it.

When I had almost finished writing the rough draft of my memoir, I discovered some postcards that I didn't remember having in my possession. As I read them, I was literally sick with grief. Strange, but while I was writing about the labour camp, I didn't remember these postcards at all. I think the postcards from my parents made me feel guilty about the way I described the years before I left. But all the same, they cannot change the past. They stirred up feelings in me that I don't fully understand.

September 19, 1940, Zduńska Wola

Dearest daughter Basia,

We received your postcard, which means you must still be doing all right. In life, one has to try to make do. With us, there is nothing new. Your mother sent you a postcard last week about the marks she is sending you, which you should receive through Mr. Kibel. I am writing again today. As soon as you receive the postcard, please send an answer back right away. With greetings from me, your father, who hopes to hear good news from you again.

~

Najkochańsza Baila

Kilka listów Ci pisałam i żadnej
odpowiedzi nie otrzymałam już
niewiem co myśleć. moje bezsen-
ne nocy moje łzy co wylewam
nie możesz sobie wyobrazić Naj-
droższa Baila proszę cię bardzo
napisz mi kilka słów co u Ciebie
słychać ty masz chociaż co jeść
li jesteś zdrowa Kochana Baila
może masz możność dostać przepustkę przyjechać do domu to
jest moje największe pragnienie
się z Tobą zobaczyć Może nie masz
na podróż to Ci przyślę pieniądze
tylko postaraj się o przepustkę
U nas Bogu dzięki wszystko w
najlepszym porządku jesteśmy
wszyscy zdrowi Fissel przyjecha
z niewoli, czuje się dobrze ukłony
od wszystkich Tulę cię kochająca

September 25, 1940, Zduńska Wola
My dearest Basia,

I have already written you a few postcards and in so many months I received only one postcard from you, from August 8. I cannot bear it anymore, every day and night I think only about you. Do I need that? But it's futile, one has to be patient; maybe a time will come that we can all be together again. Now, dear Basia, try to understand about the 40 marks that I sent you; you have to communicate with Mr. Kibel. I am giving you his address. We can get eighty 2-kilogram loaves of bread for 40 marks. For the 40 marks we sent you, make sure to get the equivalent of 160 kilograms of bread rather than getting the value of the currency exchange – here you wouldn't get anything for this money. Write right away and tell me how you dealt with it. If you need more, write and I will send you another few marks. When I get an answer from you, then Kibel's mother will get the 40 marks because they are with a third party.
[Kibel's address in Russian follows]

From your mother, who misses you very much and wants to see you soon.

~

I don't recall the name Kibel at all. I can't recall whether I got in touch with him or not. Did I get the money? It drives me crazy that I can't remember getting it. But the idea on their part was excellent. What must have taken place was that this Mr.Kibel had a mother back home who needed help. Money was evaluated by the amount of bread you could buy with it. So if she could buy 160 kilograms of bread there, I would get the amount from him that could buy 160 kilograms of bread here.

~

October 23, 1940, Zduńska Wola
My beloved Basia,

I thank you for your dear postcard. A postman brought the card on Saturday while we were eating. I couldn't stop crying, so no one ate any more dinner. Thank God, we aren't lacking for food. We only lack for you, my dear. At every meal I say, Basia probably doesn't have this, and then I just cannot eat anymore. Today I received your second postcard. Almost everyone was at home. Herman, Fela, Łajka, and Yacov read your postcard with great joy. Thank God, it is a little better than the first one. Next time we'll send you a letter and everyone will add a line. I am surprised that you haven't yet received those 40 marks. Write and tell us how he paid you, whether it was according to the currency or, like here, according to the price of bread as I wrote you in the postcards. Can you at least get something for the money? As soon as it's possible, I will send you more. You ask how I am managing. Certainly things would be better with you here. You ask if Fela is helping us – with what? She doesn't have time to help us with work and financially we don't need it. She bought me a nice sweater. Ah, how much I would like to send it to you. Fishel and Abraham are working.

From your mother, who wishes to see you as soon as possible.

〜

November 11, 1940, Zduńska Wola
My dearest Basia,

After much suffering, I finally received a postcard from you. Your writing has made us very happy. Thank God you are healthy and life has hope…. You deserved a little penance for not having listened to your parents. I begged you; I cried for you to stay home. You didn't want to listen. We are all at home, including your older brothers. Thank God we don't lack for food. But I weep over every meal. Every morsel is poisoned for me because you, my dearest, don't have it. But I have to live with the hope that you'll be with us again. Then you will listen to us, won't you? Every day is like a year to me – waiting so many years for you is terrible. I am now living with the Marguleses. We weep together, as they also have a daughter where you are, and they also receive good letters. Now, dear Basia, I am sending you another 40 marks. You will receive them from Mr. Kibel – you know him well. Thirty marks are from us and 10 are from Fela. I am including his address [follows in Russian]. *Tomorrow I will send you another postcard, from Fela as well. Daddy will write the next one.*

Your loving mother.

～

I feel terrible. I cannot recall the Marguleses, neither the parents nor the daughter. Is it possible that during this particular period my mind was partially blurred or obstructed by the enormous physical and emotional stress?

～

November 26, 1940, Zduńska Wola
Dearest daughter Basia,

Your postcard has filled us with joy. We are in really good health. It is still warm here and I hope the rest of the winter won't be much colder. There is very little coal here. We have heard there have already been serious frosts where you are. We have to get used to everything. Have you received the money? You didn't get enough in the exchange.

With greetings from me, your father, who hopes to see you again.

～

November 26, 1940, Zduńska Wola
Beloved Basia,

Thank you for your postcard. Thank God you are sounding a little better now. Forgive me for not writing to you for so long but I couldn't. A boarder moved in with us, into the kitchen. Imagine what a disarray it is. The Markowiczs live in the last room, we are in the middle and Lewkowicz lives in the kitchen. I can't manage in this confined space. My dear, have you already received the money from Kibel? Maybe you requested too little money in relation to bread? Here a kilogram of bread costs 25 pfennigs. Maybe you asked for too little; you can request more from him because he wrote to his mother asking her to let him know what one can buy here for one mark. So apparently he doesn't want to take advantage of you. I have already paid Mrs. Kibel the 40 marks. Dear Basia, write to let us know if you need our help. We will send you what we can, although it is difficult now because none of the children have work. But in any case, if you need it, I will send you as much as I can so my heart will be lighter. Thank God things are all right here and we are healthy. One can get everything for money. But things are very bad where Aunt Sara lives; many people simply starve to death. Everyone will write to you this week. I bought 5 or 6 postcards.

From your longing mother. I am awaiting your reply.

⌣

Winter came – with a big, heavy snow and steady temperatures of minus 20 to 30 degrees Celsius. We were given special quilted clothes and boots. The days had grown very short, so we had to get up in the dark and come home at dark. Many people had frozen toes and fingers and began to show signs of poor nutrition. Many were getting sick and weren't given much medical help. Our diet wasn't balanced and there weren't any fruits or vegetables, although I thought that the oatmeal cereal in the morning was the tastiest food I ever ate. The bread was dark, mostly with sand crunching under our teeth, but even that we didn't get enough of. Everybody complained, but nobody paid attention to us.

⌣

December 19, 1940, Zduńska Wola
My dearest Basia,

I don't know why you don't write. I don't know what to think anymore. It is very cold here. I can imagine how cold it must be where you are, how you, my dearest, must be suffering. Dear Basia, write me everything, all your sufferings. Who can you tell about your worries and pains if not your mother? Who will listen more than your mother? Even though I cannot help you, I would like to share in your suffering even from afar. Dear Basia, write me everything. Did you at least get some warm clothing? Do you at least have enough to eat? I don't stop thinking about you even for a minute. I keep thinking about how you must be freezing. My dear, let me know if you have already received the money from Kibel. Did you ask him to add some more because you requested too little? A kilogram of bread costs 28 pfennigs here. My dear, write and let me know how much of our help you need. Don't feel embarrassed. I will send you as much as we can, although things are difficult here now – there isn't any work – but I will send the money to you anyway. It will make my heart lighter. There is no news here; we are all healthy. We are now experiencing very difficult times here, but I would still be content with everything if you, my dearest, were at home. But it's futile, all we can do is suffer and wait until the time comes when we will all be together. I hope that I will still be alive to see that. They were saying that our uncle would come and that you could come also, so we were all very happy – but our uncle doesn't seem to be coming.

Regards from your longing mother. Regards from the entire family.

$$\sim$$

I think by "uncle" she is referring to the Soviets. There must have been rumours about war between Germany and the Soviet Union, and they must have thought that if the Soviets advanced into Poland, I would be able to come home. How sad.

$$\sim$$

January 7, 1941, Zduńska Wola
My dearest Basia,

After much torment I received your postcards, one after another. I didn't know what to think; for 6 weeks I hadn't received any word from you. Imagine my suffering – I couldn't sleep. Imagine our joy when I received your postcard and another one a few days later. Everyone who was at home cried when I read your card. Herman and Fela were here too. You asked if I remember when we said goodbye on Piłsudskiego

Street. I can tell you there has not been a day that I haven't thought of you and talked about you. I talk about you the most at our Saturday meals and I can't stop crying. But it's futile; I have to be patient and wait until you come, wait for the time when we are all together again. I hope that I live long enough to see this happy moment and to see you again. Thank God things are better for you now – it makes me very happy that you don't have to work in the forests anymore in such terrible cold. It is very cold here and I can only imagine how cold it is where you are, how you must be suffering, my dear. Does the place where you are cleaning pay you living expenses? Write and tell me everything. Dear Basia, you wanted Mordka's address; you probably remember the name of the town, so I will only write down the street. We are going to have our photographs taken tomorrow and I'll send you a copy for Mordka. If you receive an answer from him, send it to us. We haven't had any news from him. Pinas Herzl Street.

From your loving mother, C. Kohn.

Please respond right away and send us a picture of you. Regards from everyone.

~

The irony of it would almost be funny if it wasn't so sad. I had to be careful what I wrote and so did they. When I told her I cleaned floors, she assumed that I was a maid or housekeeper. Naturally this would have been a dream for me too since it would have meant that I got room and board. I understood that they couldn't communicate with anybody except for people in the Soviet Union as long as the neutrality pact with Germany was in effect. This was the reason that she didn't mention Palestine or Haifa, where my brother lived.

~

Early one evening in the new year, 1941, a strange thing happened while I was standing outside with a group of people. It was the custom in Poland to shake hands whenever people meet or part. One of the boys said to me, "Come on, don't you see my hand?" I didn't realize it at first, but it was true – I hadn't seen his hand. The next day I went to the doctor and he told me that I had developed night blindness due to a lack of certain vitamins. There was no medication available, so the doctor prescribed raw onions from the kitchen. This sounds like a joke, but it's true. It really came as a shock to me. Here I was, still having steady high temperatures and now I had developed night blindness. I was scared and lonely, especially after visiting my friend Bluma in the hospital. I experienced moments of weakness and a voice inside me was crying, "I can't take it anymore" while another voice in me kept saying, "No, you must go on. Remember that you are a survivor."

At about this same time another incident occurred during an inspection by some high authorities from Arkhangelsk. After all, we were foreign citizens and the Soviets needed to adhere to at least some rules. Everything in the camp was cleaned and scrubbed. Before the authorities arrived, good food was stocked in the kitchen, and plenty of it. Everybody worked shorter hours. It was a major preparation. This started me thinking that if this was the case, if the local authorities went to such lengths to hide the real conditions in the camp from their superiors, then they must have taken it upon themselves to treat us in whatever way they wanted. They were probably stealing the food that was meant for us. When we were all gathered outside for the inspection, I stood there, listening, and nobody from our group said anything. I was boiling inside; I felt as if I would explode. As the senior authorities started walking away, I ran after one of them who was a little older, closer I would say to forty, and fine-looking. In my far-from-perfect Russian, I managed to get his attention and told him that every day was not like this, that it had all been prepared for them. He didn't say anything. I told him that I had been running a high temperature for weeks, and that my girlfriend was dying from tuberculosis. He told me to come to their quarters.

Well, my friends were shocked. They thought that I would probably be sent away to a much tougher camp, that I'd never survive. I didn't say anything and went to the authorities' office where the man was waiting for me. He told me that he would make arrangements for me to go to the hospital in the big city where we had first arrived and be thoroughly checked out. Needless to say, I was relieved. It confirmed my belief once again that one has to speak up for oneself. I was the hero of the camp for awhile.

The authorities made all the arrangements and I went to the city where I spent a very nice few days in the hospital. It was like staying in a resort. I was even allowed to walk around the streets between tests. I had my freedom for a few days and, even better than that, the official invited me to his house one evening for supper with his family. The doctors prescribed some medication for me and I was sent back to the camp. As for the conditions there, nothing changed.

~

February 18, 1941, Zduńska Wola
My beloved Basia,

Thank you for your postcard, which delighted us immensely. You write that you want me to send you a parcel. It is impossible – we can't send any parcels. I would love to send you one even though our material situation has changed a lot. The children haven't been able to earn anything for three months. Since that time, everything has been taken away from us, and there is no work. We don't have any property to sell, so we still need whatever cash we have left. One needs to make peace with this fate. It is much worse where Aunt Sara lives. Thank God we have enough potatoes for the entire winter, and so far we haven't lacked for bread. People who have money can get everything. One wears what one has, though. Even the greatest intelligentsia here have to wear clogs; there is no shame. Everyone is waiting for these times to pass and to live to see better times. Everyone is living in very cramped situations, with several families living in one apartment. At our place, one man lives in the kitchen and, as you know, Milka lives in the last room. Who knows whether they will shove someone else in our place. We have very little furniture left, mostly beds. That's how we live…. My dear, why do you write so little about yourself? What illness did you suffer from? Now I have that to worry about. Are you completely healthy now? Send us your picture. Is it possible? I will try to send you a family photo. When you get a letter from Mordka, forward it to us.

Your mother C. Kohn.

⌒

I must have hoped that my parents could send me some medication. I didn't specify what. I just wanted to know if it was possible for them to send anything to us.

⌒

March 6, 1941, Zduńska Wola
Dear Basia,

Although I hadn't received a letter from you for such a long time, I calmed down because of the postcard that Fela received from you. You wrote that you were ill. What was the matter? Where were you staying while you were sick? Do you at least have bedding? Is it warm enough there? Are you completely healthy? Thank God you have a place where you are in service. Be patient and stay there longer, at least until spring. Are you there to make a living? It made me very happy to hear that you were able to buy yourself something because here, forget about it. My dear, let us know what you did about the registration. Where did you sign up to go? The Margules girl wrote that she signed up to come home, so her mother is very anxious. Basia, don't you remember the town where Mordka lives? Send us a letter from Mordka. Please answer. Mordka Chajfa Pinas Herzl Street.

⌒

I'm not sure what registration my mother is talking about – they must have been getting very different information. This was only March

1941 and the war between Germany and the Soviet Union didn't break out until June – that was when the Soviet government allowed us to go where we wanted. The Margules girl couldn't possibly have registered to go home to Poland at this point – perhaps she was referring to the earlier registration, in 1940. At any rate, my mother clearly didn't want me to come home anymore. She asked if I remembered where my brother Mordechai lived. She was giving me a clue that I should register to go to Palestine. I can see more and more how much we were all kept in the dark, on both sides. I can't help but chuckle about my mother's advice to stay on at my housekeeping job until spring. If only she knew. My writing was also very unclear; I knew that everything was being censored. We could only write postcards to make the censors' job easier. My mother was happy that I could buy myself something new. I did buy a new pair of felt boots called *valenkye* – my old ones had holes in them and my feet were freezing – so I must have used the money I got from them for this purpose.

⁓

By the time spring 1941 arrived, Bluma was getting worse. She had shrunk to the size of a little girl and lost her hair – almost all I could see was her big, blue eyes. I was really fond of her and seeing her like this was heartbreaking. A few days after my last visit to her, she died. They notified me and drove me to the small hospital. It was in another camp like ours and I usually walked there. I claimed her body and had to sign some documents. They put her in a plain, long coffin, like a wooden crate, put it on top of a carriage with two horses and a driver. The Russian guard and I had to sit on top of the coffin since there was no other room, and this was how I brought Bluma's body back for burial. I am writing about this so matter-of-factly now, but it was a terrible tragedy for me and for the whole camp. The funeral was a very dramatic experience for all of us – Bluma's life was so tragically cut short. She had been so young and beautiful. A mood of resignation engulfed us all. How long were we going to be here? Who was going to be next?

But life went on. There was no time for prolonged mourning. We couldn't afford the luxury of deep feelings. There was the next day, the next moment to deal with.

～

April 14, 1941, Zduńska Wola
My dearest Basia,

I don't know what to think anymore. It has been several months since I received a letter from you. But I calmed down a little when I saw a card from you at the Karpens' and received word from the Marguleses that you were at their daughter's place and the two of you took a picture together. But I cannot wait for you to send us this picture. Ah, I would so love to see you at least in a picture, to see what you look like. I was a bit embarrassed that you wrote to others and not to us. What does it mean? Are you upset with us? I don't understand. How are you? Are you healthy? Are you working? Write and tell me everything. Yosef wrote that he is trying to arrange for you to live at his place; this would be so good. Have you written to Mordka? When you receive an answer, forward it to us because I haven't had any news from him and would very much like to hear from him. There is nothing new with us – we are all healthy. We now have four families living in our place. I'd be rich if they were really tenants, wouldn't I? I kiss you. Please answer right away.

Your mother C. Kohn.

～

The Yosef she mentions was the younger brother of my brother-in-law, who had also escaped from Poland when I did. He went to the Soviet Union voluntarily in 1940, rather than registering to go back to Poland, and lived in freedom – at least as much as most Soviet citizens did. This was the last postcard I received from my family. I had an eerie feeling – it didn't sound as if it had been written by the same woman. I could sense that she was hiding a lot from me, that she was on the verge of a breakdown. Her ending to this last letter was different than any of the others: "I kiss you, please answer right away, your mother." This was her final goodbye and I wondered why it was so cold and detached. It wasn't until years later that I got my answer.

~

The summer of 1941 arrived. We were already dreading the coming winter, but before it arrived fate came into play yet again and caused a tremendous change in my little world. Up to this point we had had no connection with the outside world and the guards gave us no news at all. Even if they had been willing to share what they knew, their news was so censored and so altered that it wouldn't have made much difference.

Then, one morning, there was excitement among the guards. Something big had clearly taken place, but what? Finally, there was a public announcement that Germany had declared war on the Soviet Union. It was June 22, 1941. To the great bewilderment of the guards, we were overwhelmed with joy and started singing and dancing. They stared at us as if we had gone berserk. Our reaction to the terrible news was a mystery to them. All I can say to explain it is that when there seems to be no hope, change is better than nothing.

As it turned out, though, this event did have a positive effect on us. A few days after the first announcement, the authorities told us that we were free to go wherever we wanted within the Soviet Union – the Soviet government had granted us amnesty. They would even provide our transportation and food. After the first shock subsided, we had a big decision to make – where should we go? How would we even decide? We didn't know anything about conditions in the different parts of the Soviet Union. Some people were more informed, but nobody really knew the truth about this closed society. So what were we to do? People formed groups they wanted to travel with and then each group decided on a destination. The guards in the office put up a big map of the Soviet Union and gave us the privilege of staring at the lines, dots and different colours – but what did it tell us? Nothing.

In my own group were Hela and her sister, Lola; Ala and her brother, Heniek, from Warsaw; Feiga from Wilno; David and the two Wrublewski brothers from Lodz; Lola from Warsaw; and, from my town, Adela, Abraham and Henry Sztainhorn, Srulek Lipman and Aaron Leibowicz. We held meeting after meeting, but couldn't arrive at any decision that was acceptable to the whole group. Then I, the youngest, came up with a brilliant idea – since we were so far north, why not go far south, to the Caucasus Mountains, to the Black Sea, where there was no winter? Everyone agreed on that. But we had to give the authorities the name of a specific town. Again, I looked at the map. This was the time of Stalin's regime and I knew that he was born in Gori, which I thought had to be an old town. Next to Gori I saw a town named Staliniri. "This is it," I said. "It's named after Stalin and it's next to Gori, about twenty kilometres away."

Everybody agreed that Staliniri would be our next stop. It sounded nice and at least it was going to be warm. For the next few weeks, we were busy with various preparations such as health examinations and filling out paperwork. The fear of the unknown never entered our minds.

If I counted how many places I have lived, all my different addresses, I'm curious what number I would come up with. In our modern, North American society, there is a high level of stress connected with change, even with moving within the same city. Is there a stress level count for all the many changes I went through, I wonder?

South to Georgia

For our trip down south, we were given a ticket that was actually just a pass to our destination – the means of getting there was up to us. We soon found out that we couldn't take a plane. I lost count of how many train stations we slept in during our more than 3,000-kilometre journey south and how many trains we rode on. In spite of it all, our spirits were high. We were even joking and laughing, not really afraid of what the future might hold. At least we were free.

We passed through the real Soviet Union and we witnessed a people who looked as if they accepted their fate completely passively, with total resignation on their faces. We didn't communicate with anyone on our way, though. First of all, we looked different, conspicuous, and therefore suspicious, and we still didn't speak Russian very well.

The war was already apparent – we saw soldiers everywhere. The railway stations were filled with them and we could see long trains packed with army personnel. But aside from the war, which was just beginning, the sight of Soviet travellers, with their sad, grey, expressionless faces, was something I, for one, had never seen before. The railway station was full of travellers and everybody carried food with them, since no one ever knew when their train would arrive. We sometimes slept on the same station floor for two to three days, but at least we were now equal with the Soviet people because we were free.

It took us six weeks to arrive in Staliniri, tired but full of hope. In retrospect, it seems very odd to me that we didn't even think about the war and our families in Europe on this trip – the present, I guess, was too absorbing. There was no mental energy left to deal with much more. As we moved south, we could see the differences in the regions of the Soviet Union and approaching Georgia was actually almost like getting out of the USSR.

The Georgians were dark-haired, beautiful men and women. They dressed much more attractively; there wasn't the same greyness and the sadness on faces that we saw elsewhere in the Soviet Union. Georgian people speak Georgian, their own language – it was one of several states that had been part of the Russian Empire that were conquered by the Soviet Red Army and forced to join the Union of Soviet Socialist Republics in 1921 after a few short years of independence. I came to understand them very well and developed many friendships among the local people. Staliniri was actually in South Ossetia, a small state within Georgia. I wasn't aware of this when I first arrived.

We arrived at the city hall in Staliniri to register ourselves on a beautiful day in October 1941. The small town of about 30,000 was fairly new, neat and clean, consisting of small private homes and some public office buildings. The local authorities officially greeted us. We were somewhat of a sensation to them since we came from such a different world. There were some local Jewish families who came to see us, but we couldn't communicate with them at all. They didn't speak Yiddish, although some were very religious and knew the language of the Bible. We didn't understand either of their two languages – Russian and Georgian – very well so we could only communicate by gesturing.

They took us to an orchard full of grapes, bananas and oranges and we went wild, picking the beautiful fresh fruits. Some of us ate so much that we got sick. Georgia exported fruit to the rest of the Soviet Union but only party officials or people who had the money to pay for it on the black market could get it.

The next step was to find living quarters for us; in Georgia, as in all of the Soviet Union, there was no free market for living quarters. You were assigned whatever was available and there was no disputing it. By this time, the Germans were advancing quickly through the Ukraine and central Russia, and a lot of Soviets, I think mostly Jews, were running away from the Germans as we had done, so the shortage of living quarters in Staliniri was very acute. Some local families were forced to give up rooms for the *biezhenietz*.

I later met many refugees who were mostly Jews from cities such as Kiev and Minsk. I found them to be interesting, intelligent and warm people. It was easier for them to integrate because they were considered to be Soviet citizens and, accordingly, were given help. They were mostly women and children – the men were in the army or were not given permission to leave.

Feiga from Wilno and the two sisters from Kalisz, Lola and Hela, and I asked for accommodation together. We were offered a single room with a Georgian family of four – a young mother whose husband was in the army. She lived with her two small children and her parents. This particular family had a two-room house and the door that connected the two rooms was blocked off by a tall cabinet. Fortunately, there was a door leading out into the porch from each room. We were given four small narrow beds that we put against the walls on two opposite sides; a table with chairs, which was in the middle of the room; a wood-burning stove in one corner; some shelves for our few pots, pans and dishes; and some hangers on the wall for our very meagre wardrobes.

For some reason, not all the people we started out with wound up in Staliniri. Some went to other states or cities in Georgia. David was here and moved in with two other young men. In the town we came across some people like us who had arrived from different labour camps.

Our next step was to find some kind of employment, but none of us had any skills or profession – we had been too young when we left home. As I mentioned, though, the main industry here was fruit exporting, which meant that people were needed for all kind of jobs such as sorting fruit, packing and shipping. One of the two sisters got a job sorting fruits, which meant that we had more fruit than we could normally afford, although fruits were reasonably cheap here. The other sister got a job in a cloakroom in the local theatre.

Feiga and I were able to get office jobs because we had learned some Russian in the camp. I was very apprehensive about my ability to handle any kind of office work, but the local people tried to reassure me that they would help me and that I would be given the opportunity to learn the language and further my schooling, no matter where I worked. So my first position was as a secretary, or record keeper, in a high school. They had a different system here than in Poland – students either went to school for seven years before entering a *tekhnikum*, or vocational school, or they went straight through a nine-year program to prepare for college or university. I worked in the latter type of school. The majority of the teachers in our school were women, at least in the lower grades. The math and science teachers were usually men.

I began to realize that the South Ossetian people were different than Georgians. Their way of thinking was, in general, closer to our European way than was true for other people in the Soviet Union; to me they seemed more culturally and intellectually refined, whereas the Georgians evoked a more powerful presence. My first and most important aim was to adapt to the new environment – to the people, culture and language – and to learn as much as I possibly could. Mostly I wanted to understand the people, both the locals and the refugees. I had plenty of opportunities to mingle with both groups. I also met the rest of our Jewish refugee community, which, I would guess, numbered about forty or fifty people. We used to meet for picnics sometimes, but in the beginning we mostly kept company with David and his two roommates.

David worked in a big fruit-drying plant and used to bring us delicious dried pears, prunes and nectarines. We spent time together but the two of us were never alone. It was a very strange friendship – our "romantic" involvement consisted of him sitting on my bed and talking sometimes. Strangely, I still didn't have any particular feelings for him one way or another. I think he was rather shy and introverted. He was always very polite and proper, but he simply didn't have the skills to court a girl. It's important to realize that we didn't start our teenage years the way young people do in North America. This part of our growing up was cut short, affected by our new experiences and, even more so, by our fight for survival.

Lola, the older of the two sisters, was the head of our group. As I've said, she was quite a bit older than us and was a very disciplined, strict, good worker – a no-nonsense person. We soon settled into our new lives: everyone went to work in the morning and then prepared very plain meals after work on the wood-burning stove. We had to buy the wood from the market. Cleaning was done by any of us, as there wasn't too much to do.

Here again, just as I had in the years back home, I began to build a world of my own; it wasn't by design, it just happened slowly. My friends didn't have enough to offer me and I felt that I had to reach out somewhere else. There was no problem doing it here. In the la-bour camp, I hadn't had many options – I had had to stay put. There was nowhere to go and life was too harsh to even think of much else besides passing the day.

Now, in the school, my workplace, there was a new world of dis-covery, of growing and learning. Right from the start they assigned me a teacher of Russian as a tutor. She was a very beautiful woman in her early twenties, a native Ossetian and the daughter of a university professor from a very prominent family. Her name was Aza and she was the first friend I made there. She invited me to her house, which, compared to our one room, was luxury. They had three or four rooms that were nicely furnished and very clean. I met her mother, a real lady, and her brother. I asked about her father and here, for the first time, I was confronted with a very common phenomenon in the

Soviet Union – they told me that he was in a jail or labour camp. I
didn't know how to react. For me, coming from a non-Communist
country, it was rare to know anyone who had relatives in jail. It was
unthinkable. As I found out from Aza, and from many more people
later, one could be arrested in the Soviet Union for no reason. These
people were officially labelled enemies of the Communist state or of
the revolution, and were sent to Siberia without any trial, sometimes
never to be seen or heard from again.

I also became friends with Zamira, an arithmetic teacher in the
lower grades. She was strikingly beautiful, dark-haired with grey-
green eyes, tall and rather reserved, with an enigmatic smile. While
Aza was sweet and vivacious and very intelligent, Zamira, who wasn't
very strong intellectually, was very sensuous and feminine.

Another new friend was Helena, the physical education teacher, a
blond who was a mixture of Russian and Georgian. There were some
blond Georgians, too, although it was rare. Helena was totally different from the others. She was more down-to-earth than either Aza
or Zamira, with a pixie-like kind of beauty; I liked to be with her
because she was refreshing in her simplicity.

Elena was a history teacher in the higher grades. She came from
a mixed background and was a different type of person entirely. She
was rather mysterious and I could never really figure her out. There
was so much depth to her, it was no wonder I was drawn to her. I
tried to spend as much time with her as I could. She could be found
buried in novels by Tolstoy or Dostoyevsky; she was slow-moving
and slow-talking and serious most of the time, and looked straight
at you with her big, sad eyes. I had the feeling that inside this calm
and collected exterior was a woman capable of great passion, ready to
be ignited and set on fire. We became very close friends and used to
confide in each other.

I also became friendly with the principal of the school, but only
to a certain point. She was a young Ossetian woman in her early
thirties, I think. She taught English and had finished university in

Leningrad. There were some differences between graduates from a Georgian university and those from one of the Russian universities such as Leningrad or Moscow. She was more distant than the rest of them, but not because of her position – I found out later that she had just come out of an unhappy personal relationship.

My work at the school was actually very boring and I could do it in two hours, so the rest of the day I worked on my Russian assignments and began English lessons with the principal. I began to integrate into the new environment and some of my new girlfriends used to come to our place to visit me. They were curious about my life here and of course about my life up to now. My roommates didn't mind them – meeting these women was something new and different for them too.

The ongoing war hadn't touched us directly yet, but it robbed us of our peace of mind. We knew that we weren't suffering the way people suffered back home, but the postcards I had received in the camp hadn't given me the impression that their lives were threatened. All communication with the rest of the world had been disrupted with Germany's attack on the Soviet Union in June 1941. All we could do was go about our lives and wait until we could go home, whenever that might be. In a way, fate took pity on us: it would have been impossible to go on with the devastating knowledge of what was actually happening in Poland. Sometimes ignorance can be bliss.

When the 1942 school year came to an end and summer vacation was approaching, there was a tenth-grade graduation party in the cafeteria. I sat with the teachers even though I wasn't much older than the graduates. They were around seventeen and eighteen; by that time I was nineteen. The students were nice kids who worked hard and took school seriously. They were involved in different activities and some of them were in the Communist Youth Union, the Komsomol. The average family here had no more than one child – two was a rarity.

At the graduation party, there were speeches by the principal, some of the teachers and some representatives from the board of education of South Ossetia. As I sat there listening to them, I couldn't help but feel sorry for myself. Why was I so often denied so much? Why had I been robbed of my teenage years? Something suddenly prompted me to raise my hand and ask to speak. I was unprepared, really not knowing what to do or what I wanted to convey to the young people. The teachers let me talk and the words just poured out of me, unrestrained. I told them that I hoped they appreciated their young years, their opportunities ahead, and would try to make the best of their lives. I hadn't been so privileged in my life – fate had thrown me far away from my home and my parents. Well, there was total silence. I really didn't see anybody – it was as if I was there alone; my words had come out very easily, as if it was someone else speaking. It was the applause that brought me back to reality. I hadn't expected that kind of reaction. The students were touched and the teachers were surprised by my knowledge of Russian and my ability to express what I felt so well. Everybody came over to congratulate me and somebody gave me a bouquet of flowers. I was the celebrity of the evening.

Following that event, the people from the board of education took an interest in me and asked me to work in the state building where the board had their offices. I wasn't qualified for any specific position, but there was always room for somebody in their bureaucracy. They put me in the planning department, to be trained by the supervisor. So I moved to an office in the tallest, nicest building in town. It was a new environment, with new people to meet. There wasn't much challenge in this strictly clerical type of work, though, just charts and charts, and numbers and figures. The people I worked with were just as uninteresting as the work. I knew I wouldn't last very long there. Meanwhile, another event took place that disturbed me for quite some time and caused me many sleepless nights.

While I was leaving work one day, a man handed me a note. The local NKVD, the secret police, had called me to appear at their offices one evening. The note gave me the time and place and included one more sentence: "It is in your best interest not to tell anybody about this." I was shocked, mystified and horrified. What would the NKVD, the most feared organ of the State, want from me? I hadn't committed any crime and I wasn't involved in anything criminal. I was perplexed.

The day of my appointment arrived. It was eight o'clock in the evening. I handed in the note at the front desk and somebody ushered me into a room that was lit by only one small lamp. It was pretty dark and I could hardly make out the face of the man sitting behind a massive desk. The very atmosphere in the room scared me. I walked in slowly and shyly and the man behind the desk motioned to me to sit down in front of his desk. I saw a very pleasant face, Ossetian, middle-aged, maybe forty or older. "Don't be afraid," he said. "You haven't committed any crime and it's not you we are after. We just need your help."

It turned out that they knew that some of the people in our community were involved in so-called black marketeering and they had picked me to get to know what everybody was doing and to keep them informed. In other words, I was to betray my friends. I just listened – I didn't know how to react or what to say, so I kept quiet. He was ahead of me, as if reading my mind, and said, "There is nothing for you to say. You have no choice in the matter." I left in silence, the way I came, just bewildered. Why me? What was I going to do? I couldn't even talk to anybody about it. They gave me a week until the next meeting.

From the very beginning, I knew that I wouldn't do it. I wouldn't be the one to condemn any of my friends – or anyone else, for that matter – to an indefinite term in the toughest hard labour camps. I knew what people were involved in, which to us was plain trading, not stealing or cheating, and certainly not a crime that deserved such cruel punishment as life imprisonment. The question was how I could find a way to get out of it and what the repercussions would be if I refused. I didn't want to ask him, in case I got scared and gave in, so I just kept thinking. In my desperation, my inner struggle was consuming me, leaving me unable to work or concentrate. Why was fate testing my strength so often? It was so unfair. In my nightmares, I visualized myself being despised by all of my people and most likely chased away as a traitor, unworthy of their trust. I saw myself alone, devastated by guilt and shame if I collaborated with the NKVD. It would come out eventually, but even if it didn't, I wouldn't be able to live with myself. If I could only talk to my girlfriends about it…. But I was afraid that they would wonder why the NKVD had picked me and suspect me no matter what. So I kept silent and continued to torment myself. My friends could tell that something was wrong but I told them that I had had a few very unpleasant encounters at work and they believed me. It sounded probable – they knew I happened to be very sensitive to the way people treated me.

For the second meeting with the NKVD, I gave the excuse that I hadn't had a chance to get together with anybody because I wasn't feeling well. He believed me. This went on for about three weeks until finally I decided that I would talk to him on a different level. I would try to make him understand me and try to touch his heart. What was in my favour was that I found out that he was the father of one of the students I knew, a boy in the graduating class who had heard my emotional speech. I hoped this would somehow save me.

I prepared myself mentally and planned what I was going to say. I had nothing to lose. I told him about his son, who was close to my age. I told him to ask his son if he remembered me. Didn't he think I had enough to cope with alone during the war, away from everybody at the other end of the world, not knowing whether I would ever see my family again? Would he like his son to be burdened with a guilt of this magnitude for the rest of his life? There was silence for a change on the other side of the desk. He looked at me very intently, digesting what he heard. I could almost feel his inner turmoil and, after a while – which felt like an eternity – he said, "Okay, my child. Go home, but never tell anybody about what happened here. You may get me into trouble." I have never walked so fast in my life.

~

We heard various vague reports about the war. The papers and the radio gave us news that was heavily censored – the broadcasters and journalists were told exactly what information to release to the public – and only mentioned shortages of food and that the army came first. One day I heard in the office that the board of education was offering a course in accounting or bookkeeping specifically designed for a *kolkhoz*, a cooperative farm. There were many of these around South Ossetia, some not far from Staliniri. I got a brilliant idea and I told my roommates about it. I would go to work on a farm and that way, we would be able to get enough food. I needed some money to pay for the course and had to get their approval. They agreed.

The course took place in a school in the evening since we all worked during the day. There were about forty people, mostly women, who were taking the course for the same reason that I was. To my great surprise, I saw Zamira, one of the teachers I had become friendly with while working at the high school.

Just as we sat down, in walked the most handsome Georgian, in his thirties or older, dressed in a colonel's uniform. He was a professor of political science and economics at the University of Tbilisi, the capital of Georgia and had been given a year's leave of absence to teach bookkeeping in our small town. I guess that he must have had some pull to get this assignment, away from the army, during the war. The army uniform made him look even more impressive. I saw him later in a civilian suit and he was still handsome, but the uniform definitely added another dimension to his looks. He was a replica of Stalin but slimmer and taller; he had nice features with the same black hair, moustache and dark black, penetrating eyes. I was instantly attracted to him, as were all the other girls and women in the class. They were all local and I was the only foreigner. I felt kind of unnoticed at first and I wasn't too sure of myself. I didn't feel part of the group yet – I was a stranger and very different on top of it.

Our professor's name was Levan Davidovich Ashkenadze. In Russia and the other republics, a person is called by their first name and then by a derivative of their father's name; for instance, David becomes Davidovich. I was officially called Basia Chaimovna Kohn, Chaim being my father's first name. It was difficult to get used to, but I accepted it along with many other strange customs there.

I wanted so badly to be noticed by the professor and didn't know how to go about it – it was driving me crazy. I tried very hard to do good work and handed all my homework in on time. The whole town was buzzing about the new handsome man in their midst. Even Aza, the other teacher from the high school, had heard about him. All the beautiful local girls had crushes on him. The girl I most worried about was Zamira because she was right there in the class and I know he noticed her. He couldn't help it. Another woman in the class who was hooked on him was a Jewish woman in her early forties whom I had befriended.

I had described him to my roommates and one day my friend who worked in the cloakroom of the local theatre told me that she had seen him with Zamira. My heart sank. I was filled with a jealousy that made no sense at all. I was always reaching for the stars, but now he was my star and I was obsessed with finding a way to reach him, to have him at least notice me. I started moving from the back rows to the front seat, coming earlier to school and asking questions that I really knew the answers to. He finally noticed me and one day after school asked me to help him carry our homework. He had asked Zamira once before, as well as somebody else. It reminded me of the old days in public school when the teachers asked me to help them carry our notebooks home. I was in heaven. We waited until everyone else had left and he straightened out his desk. I remember that there was one of those very rare freezing rains and since the school was on top of a hill, it was very slippery to walk down, especially in the dark. He held my arm for support and I felt as if I was already living a dream come true.

We stopped in front of the place where he lived. He had a very nice big house in Tbilisi, but here he only occupied one room with a local family. He told me to wait because it was too slippery for me to go home alone. I kind of resisted – I was embarrassed that he would ask me how many of us lived in the one room. But he left me in front of the little wooden fence outside our house.

This was the beginning of one of my most exotic, intense and beautiful love affairs, extraordinary because of the setting and the background. If one tried to write a script for it, it couldn't be any more exciting or colourful. It was never stormy like many of these kinds of relationships could be; instead, it was soft and gentle, yet so powerful.

We were from such different worlds and he was much older, by about fifteen years or so. To me he was an unattainable dream and to him I was a little girl from a world he had never seen. He was fascinated by it and, I guess, by me too. The course lasted only six months. We saw each other very often at his place and we talked a lot. He was divorced and had a twelve-year-old boy who lived with his mother. We slowly grew fonder of each other, although he was very careful not to cross certain physical boundaries, as he worried about the consequences. After all, I was a young girl away from her parents and he didn't want to hurt me.

One day he asked me to go with him to the theatre and this was more than I could have dreamt about. My roommates tried to dress me up – one gave me her nicest dress, another gave me her coat. I wished that every local girl who knew him would be there to see me with him. I can't find enough words to describe the feeling inside me; it was like nothing and nobody else existed, only the two of us. I am still thankful today for having the opportunity and capacity to feel like that. As it turned out, he felt the same way. He kept saying that he had never been so fascinated and so drawn to any other woman in his life, and I am sure he had had many experiences.

We went to the library and to the movies, but mostly for long walks. He wanted to know everything about me. I talked to him about my childhood, mostly about Hashomer Hatzair, and he was intrigued by everything.

I was a struggling young girl whose main preoccupation and most difficult battle was coping with herself. I told him that I now knew what it meant to be a Jew in a Christian society; that because it was so much more difficult for us to reach our goals, we had developed outstanding abilities to survive. I talked about leaving school and about the Great Depression and living in the midst of a tense, depressed, agitated world. I explained to him about needing something to believe in, something for which I had whole-hearted enthusiasm, and how Zionism had given me that during a particular period in my life. I explained about Zionism being the movement for Jews and for Judaism's revival, and that one of the fundamentals of Zionism is the realization that antisemitism is an illness that cannot be fought with words. It must be treated and cured at its very roots.

The more we talked, the more he realized the totally different reality I lived in. He was surprised to hear how indoctrinated I had been with socialism and communism and how much I knew about Marx, Lenin and *The Communist Manifesto*. I explained to him that the Zionist movement I belonged to was socialist at its very core. "I am glad I have this first-hand opportunity to see how it works in real life in the Soviet Union," I said, "but the problem with the communist ideal is that it looks beautiful on paper and in theory; to implement it is something else. It looks to me as though it's not easy to put it into practice. The leaders seem to forget that the ideal should serve the people, the individual; it's the other way around here. What purpose does the communist ideal serve if all the people don't feel free? They don't see a broader horizon and they are considered only as working robots that blindly come and go, who are broken in body and spirit." He agreed with me wholeheartedly.

Since I had come to Staliniri, I had had countless discussions with

Russian and Ossetian people. They trusted me enough to express their feelings freely and I heard stories that I could hardly believe. Levan also told me a lot about Stalin's purges against anyone perceived as an enemy and how whole villages had been sent away to labour camps. There was an endless number of things he wanted to know about my past. I told him about the events that had contributed to my burning desire to leave and about the period of emotional struggle filled with constant tension, fear and anxiety I had experienced before leaving my family.

We talked about his life too, a life of great achievement on one hand and great personal disappointment – with regard to his marriage – on the other. I had an advantage over him in that I was living in his world and could visualize everything he told me. My past was a constant source of fascination for him. His life had been very normal in comparison to mine. Neither of us knew where all this was going to take us, but we just had to go on. There was no way of stopping it or turning back.

Meanwhile, I changed jobs again. I hadn't liked my job at the planning department from the beginning, so the people at the board of education gave me a new opportunity to work as a secretary at a teacher's college with the privilege of attending classes and receiving personal tutoring from some of the teachers. I was delighted. My roommates and I also moved to another place – our landlady's husband had come back wounded from the war and they were given back our room. So I experienced more change, but this time for the better. I loved my work and took advantage of the learning opportunity. I worked very hard to prove myself and keep up with the material in class as much as I could.

Our accounting course was coming to an end. I finished at the top of the class and as a prize received the book that covered our course, written by Levan, with his inscription on the first page. I believed that I deserved it, that it wasn't only because of our relationship. I was very sad, to say the least, that he had to go back to Tbilisi because some other engagement had been scheduled for him there.

There was never a dull moment in our lives; we had run from the Germans in the first place, then we travelled south only because we wanted a warmer climate, never really thinking about the Germans any more. We knew that the war was still on and that the Soviets were not doing too well, but we never knew the whole truth. Then, near the end of 1942, the Germans bombed Staliniri's city hall. The shock of it in our little community was unbelievable. What were we to do now? I don't know how the townspeople reacted, nor did I want to know because I was afraid that some of them might have been only too happy to welcome a change in regime.

The bombing only lasted a short while, just half an hour or so, and nobody got hurt. There wasn't a great deal of damage, but we took it as an indication that the Germans were advancing and getting close to us. We – the Jews – would be the first victims. Communication within our group started immediately; decisions had to be made fast. There was no time to waste. The whole community of refugees, about forty or fifty people, decided unanimously to run, to go by train to the Caspian Sea and then by boat to Central Asia, to the city of Tashkent, the capital of Uzbekistan. The local authorities helped them with their plans and gave them all the assistance they could.

Things didn't go so smoothly for me or for any of my roommates, however. Lola, the older of the two sisters, was in hospital with typhoid. The rest of us decided to stay with Lola until she was well enough to travel – we couldn't leave her younger sister alone. David and his roommates were literally heartsick at the thought of leaving us.

The scene at the railway station was a dramatic experience for everybody. The goodbyes sounded so final, but each side, for different reasons, was trying to control themselves. We felt that we would never see them again and they felt even worse, as if they were leaving us in the lion's den. The three of us came home very quiet and resigned. We didn't talk about anything and didn't dare to verbalize our fears. The silence was heavy and almost unbearable.

We went about our usual routine for a few days, expecting the bombing to be repeated. There still wasn't much news and the local people kept to themselves during this tense period. We felt very alone. We visited Lola in the hospital; she was getting much better, but we didn't tell her that everyone else had left. She had heard about the bombing, but we minimized the severity of it.

And then a miracle happened: the Germans began to pull back in early 1943 and the Soviets, after the famous battle of Stalingrad, started advancing westward. The immediate danger was over for us. We didn't know until after the war what had taken place. We, along with most of the Soviet people, were kept in ignorance until the Soviets began their push forward and the radio and newspapers began to be full of victorious slogans. Their national pride was restored and their heroism instantly filled the air. Songs were written and blasted on loudspeakers all over the city.

We were happy and, to make things even better, Lola came home from the hospital. We felt badly for the others – we heard that Tashkent was overrun with Soviet refugees and that the dirt and hunger were unreal. There were rumours that people were dying of hunger in the streets.

My thoughts turned again to my professor. We were keeping in touch by phone since I was fortunate enough to have a phone in the office. Very few people had phones in their homes unless they were important people in the Communist Party. I told Levan about everything and I had his full sympathy during the ordeal. When things turned around, he said that we should celebrate. He would come to Staliniri to see me and stay a few days. I couldn't believe it. There was no commitment whatsoever between us and I didn't know at that time what we had, how to categorize our relationship. I was elated, though, that he was coming to see me. I was reassured, but still couldn't really absorb the fact that I meant so much to him. Naturally I had some fears – that maybe I should stop it before it was too late, that we were worlds apart – but I managed to suppress everything and just allowed myself to be carried away by one of the most enjoyable experiences in life – waiting for someone you really like to come to see you. The waiting alone was sheer ecstasy. No matter how long it took, it made me feel so special and made the world around me so beautiful. I loved everybody and everything. Suddenly the sky was so blue and I noticed the trees and flowers; my senses were like a finely tuned instrument.

When the day came, I was to wait for him on top of the steps of the state building where I had once worked. I saw him at the bottom and didn't even recognize him at first because he was dressed in civilian clothes. He started waving as soon as he saw me and then ran up two steps at a time. It was a public place, so our meeting had to be somewhat subdued. He looked just as handsome in a suit, but different. We got into a taxi and I asked where we were going. He answered that he was staying in a hotel. I was quiet. I had never visited anybody in a hotel nor had I ever been inside one. We went up to his room and had a proper welcoming. I was still a little apprehensive – he felt it and suggested that we go down to the dining room for dinner. After a glass or two of famous Georgian wine I began to relax and to believe that this was real, that he was sitting across the table from me. I was sure at that moment that there was nobody happier than me in the whole world.

We were oblivious to everybody around us and cherished every moment. We knew that our time together would be short – which made it even more precious. We didn't know where, when or if we would ever meet again. I was mentally and emotionally prepared for the inevitable and natural ending to the evening, but I was still somewhat disturbed, not knowing what to expect. I was afraid to be disappointed since the build-up was so great and we had waited so long. In the end, it was simple, gentle and loving – there was none of the wild, uncontrollable or premeditated behaviour one sees in the movies today. It was an expression of feelings rather than a matter of satisfying needs.

Afterward, we lay together and talked like two good friends. We didn't ask each other how we felt – there was no need for it. Our modern sex therapists tell us that we should communicate, say what we like and what we don't. This was unthinkable to me and I am sure also to him. I still insist today that there is no need to take apart something that is beautiful and natural – there is no room for an instruction manual, or for giving directions to each other while engaging in a mutual surrender and acceptance. Words interfere with the harmony of the total involvement between two people.

Then it was time for Levan to take me home. My roommates didn't question me the next day about anything; they respected my privacy. It wasn't until I came to North America that I heard so many detailed descriptions about peoples' activities, even on public television. I didn't feel the need to do it then and I still feel the same way today. I can freely talk about my feelings and emotions, but sex? What for? Shouldn't we keep something so personal to ourselves? Our modern society overplays the expectations, turns it into a merely physical act or, worse yet, some very elaborate exercise. It's impersonal. It has to stand on its own – too many techniques are being employed that leave participants empty, disillusioned and always searching for more.

Levan stayed in Staliniri for a few days. While I was at work during the day, he visited friends and we saw each other in the evenings. When he had to leave, we didn't know if we would ever meet again, but for some reason our last encounter left me more at peace with myself, glad that we had had the opportunity to get to know each other on this very intimate level. It made me feel even closer to him and I wasn't at all sorry about any of it. In fact, I felt just the opposite – that no matter what the future held, our relationship had been honest on both sides and that made it all right.

~

The girls and I started to feel more and more alone, with all our people gone. We found out that the two Sztainhorn brothers and Srulek

Lipman were in Kutaisi, a city further south in Georgia. They had heard the story about everyone leaving Staliniri and heard about me being here with three of my girlfriends, whom they knew from the labour camp in Arkhangelsk.

One day Srulek Lipman came to see me and my roommates to convince us to move to Kutaisi. It was a bigger city and there were a couple hundred of our people there. The question was what we would do there. He had talked to his roommates before he left – the fourth was Aaron Liebowicz, the blond boy I mentioned before. We really appreciated their concern. Srulek talked to us at great length about more detailed plans – how to go about moving there and what to expect when we got there. He told us that the four of them were engaged in illegal manufacturing of sewing thread spools. Henry, the older of the two Sztainhorn brothers, was very clever – he had been involved in his father's big textile factory and was familiar with different processes. He had created a small machine that could wind sewing thread on spools. The yarn was stolen from state factories and a carpenter made the wooden spools for them in his house, also illegally. The boys had to put the yarn on the spools, tie them off and wrap them in cellophane, six to a package. Soldiers travelling back and forth were buying them and selling them at black markets, wherever they happened to be. There were shortages of everything. The army needed everything and they came first. But there had been shortages of everything before the war too, as far as I had heard.

This was the story of life in the Soviet Union. Black marketeering was an accepted way of surviving, although people who engaged in it literally risked their lives by doing it. The punishment, if caught, was being sentenced to a hard labour camp – few people survived it. In reality, the black market was just a primitive way of exchanging goods without state interference and without a prescribed monetary system. Everybody knew about it and nobody was embarrassed by it. The authorities were always busy trying to uncover it, by employing an army of informers.

The four boys' standard of living was much higher in comparison to other people from our town and that helped us to make the decision to leave. Before we got there, they rented a two-room flat for us, which was already an improvement. Two of them came back to help us with the move.

Kutaisi

Kutaisi is a beautiful, picturesque city with small hills everywhere, surrounded by mountains. The climate is temperate, with no snow in the winter. Our flat was walking distance from the boys' place, situated up a hill on a winding street. The front of the house was at street level and our two rooms were in the back, with a separate entrance that we had to climb about forty steps to get to. It was surrounded by beautiful trees and we felt as though we were living in a park. In one room, we put up the four beds that also served as couches and a large table and chairs in the middle. We used the next room as the kitchen, washing area and clothing storage. This was luxury compared to the one room we had had in Staliniri. Once we had settled in, we sat down with the boys to talk about our future. The plan was that Hela and Feiga would get jobs – Hela as a seamstress and Feiga at an office – and Lola would stay home and cook for all eight of us, since the boys felt very burdened with these additional chores and were very lonely as well. I was to go over to their place every day and help them with their little enterprise.

My work involved tying off the threaded spools and packing six spools in each cellophane package. I would sometimes deliver these packages to soldiers at designated meetings – I was told beforehand when to go and who to meet with. My compensation for this would be enough to cover all our household expenses, meaning our food and shelter. We were delighted because that meant that we could buy clothes for ourselves with the money Feiga and Hela made.

We settled into very pleasant routine – every evening Lola prepared delicious food and the boys came over for dinner. It felt like a real family. There were no personal involvements amongst us at the start; although later on I think Aaron liked Hela and Srulek liked Feiga, nothing was evident then.

There was a beautiful park that was a meeting place for our Jewish-Polish community. They also had a place that served as a kind of club house, but we didn't participate in it. Our own flat served as another meeting place for many young boys and men, as well as for a few women. I found one of them, Yanka from Lvov, particularly interesting and became quite good friends with her. She had been a registered nurse before the war and was about four or five years older than me. She lived with a very attractive man who had been a tailor before the war. He wasn't on her level intellectually, but she claimed that living with him made her life easier because he had a very well-paying job as a tailor with the army. I think she liked him, though. He was older than her and had been married before the war, with a daughter who was then about five years old. As was true in many cases, his family had stayed behind – the men left on their own because small children couldn't be expected to make the dangerous journey.

There were a number of boys who were always around but it didn't affect me one way or another. I was getting used to boys paying attention to me, much more so than in my pre-war years. Before I left Staliniri, I had called Levan to tell him that I was moving and, since I wouldn't have a phone, we decided to correspond by mail. We wrote beautiful letters to each other – I kept them with me, along with a big picture of him, until I got married. Although I told David all about him after the war, I eventually tore up the picture and letters.

While I was in Kutaisi I also signed up for some evening courses so that I wouldn't completely waste my time. We had no idea how long the war was going to last or when, if ever, we would be able to go home. Some people envied our idyllic life. We often went to the local theatres – there were a few of them and the artistic level was very high.

When Levan asked me to visit him in Tbilisi, I accepted with great excitement. Tbilisi was known as the "small Paris" – it was very cosmopolitan and had a beautiful opera house. By that time, I had some nice clothes and began to feel a bit more grown up. My first trip to Tbilisi was unforgettable. Levan waited for me at the station (it was an overnight journey and I had a sleeper). It felt almost too good to be true. How lucky I was to have this handsome man waiting for me. Although I was still the little girl from nowhere, he loved me nonetheless.

Levan had taken a room in a big hotel not far from the opera house. I really felt like Cinderella, as if I would wake up and the dream would be gone. We settled into our room and then went to a restaurant where all the opera stars were; they were dressed beautifully. He seemed to know so many people and introduced me to them. They treated me with curiosity – if nothing else – but he didn't care about them. I was the important one to him. We walked the streets of Tbilisi holding hands and kissing on the street; no one in this big city paid any attention. Georgia has quite a history and he showed me all the places of interest and the historic sites. But the most memorable moments were in the opera house. I had never seen an opera in real life, only in the movies. We sat in the lounge. I didn't understand Georgian but it didn't matter – the music on stage was just an addition to what was going on inside me. I was transported to a world I had never even dreamt about. Some thirty-four years later, in 1978, I took my two children, Chuck, twenty-seven, and Susan, twenty-three, on a tour of the Soviet Union and, among other cities, we went to Tbilisi. I arranged for us to go on our own to the opera and booked the same lounge for the three of us. My son even took pictures of us there. But although my husband, David, had died in 1971, I didn't try to find out anything about Levan – a beautiful memory deserves to be left alone.

One evening, when Levan and I sat in the opera house lounge, the curtain went up and the orchestra began playing, but the actors danced in silence. I quietly asked Levan when they would start singing. He didn't laugh at my ignorance and only said that he would explain later, that this was ballet. So, on this one trip, I was introduced to both opera and ballet for the first time. Today, whenever I see a performance, I can't help but recall this man and think about how many things he helped me experience.

I saw Levan in Tbilisi maybe three or four times, sometimes for a week or more at a time, and then the inevitable question came up. What would happen when the war was over? Would I leave him? I had been dreading this question; I knew that it had to come. When it did, I didn't even ask for time to think; I had to be honest. Just like that I said, "I must go home. I must see what has happened to my family." The same way that I knew I had to leave Poland when the war broke out, there was no doubt in my mind that I would have to return. He suggested that we could get married and move to Moscow, where he could easily get a position at the university. Maybe life there would be different for me than it was in Georgia. He didn't understand that if I stayed, I would never be able to leave the Soviet Union, never be able to see my friends and family again. I would feel like a prisoner. That is what the Soviet Union actually felt like to me and to others like me. As much as he understood me, and was never a believer in Communism himself, he was born there and he didn't know any other way of life. He just couldn't feel the way I did. It was very sad for both of us. We parted and decided not to see each other again because it would be too hard for both of us.

We kept up our correspondence, though. While we never touched on the painful dilemma we faced, I told him about events in Kutaisi and he wrote about what was happening with him. I felt a terrible loss – first I had lost Chaim, the young man in Kuźnica, and now Levan, although I can't compare them. My loneliness returned. Although I was surrounded by friends, I felt no deep connection to them. Levan still filled my thoughts, but I had to slowly push them away and go on with my life. I had to force myself to wait for tomorrow, for whatever was in store for me.

As it turned out, fate wanted me to be tested once again. Like so many times before, I was about to face a huge challenge. One Monday morning, as usual, I went to the boys' quarters and saw that the door was open. The place was a mess – everything was turned upside down – and nobody was there. At first, I thought that they had been robbed, but if that was the case, where were they? I walked out in disbelief and their landlord told me that he had seen the boys being handcuffed and taken away by the police. My heart almost stopped beating. I couldn't utter a word. I didn't cry; I didn't scream. I felt the way I had when my girlfriend Bluma died. I realized what must have taken place: somebody had informed the police about them. But who? The Georgians wouldn't do it and for sure none of the neighbours would – they were all involved in some kind of black marketeering. I went home and told Lola about it and we waited until the other two girls came home from work.

We sat there as if we were in mourning. We were sure that we would never see them again. People from our community heard about what had happened and came by to console us. It was a black Monday. I spoke very little, but my mind kept working. Perhaps the boys meant even more to me than I had thought. I had shared so much with them – they were like my brothers. I couldn't sleep for days. The first thing I did was to try to find out where they were being held. When I found out where they were, I kept going there and hanging around for hours. I didn't even know what for. I walked around the corridors of the main police station in Kutaisi. There were different departments that dealt with particular offences. I didn't even know which one would be in charge of their case, but I kept watching every official that passed by me, hoping that my instincts would tell me something.

One day, the police came to interrogate us. They seemed to know everything. They even knew that the boys came here for dinner every day. We admitted to that but denied any knowledge of their activities. They threatened to take us in to make a statement at the police station and sign an affidavit. If the boys had admitted that we were involved, we would be in big trouble. What were we to do? We were scared, but I said, no matter what, we should not admit to anything. The girls agreed. Days went by and I felt so helpless, sad and frustrated.

Suddenly, good fortune came my way. Since I came from the same town as the boys (whoever betrayed us must have known us well), the police called me in for questioning. I didn't know what would happen – the girls were afraid that the police would arrest me too, but somehow I wasn't scared. I had a strong feeling that everything would be all right. When I got to the police station, I very calmly walked into the office to find a middle-aged Georgian man sitting behind the desk. I couldn't help but be reminded of my encounter with the NKVD in Staliniri. The Georgian officer had a very good-natured, open kind of a face. He was of medium height and a little bit on the stout side, but fine-looking. He looked to be the right age to have children my age and I immediately thought, well, I am going to explore this avenue – it worked before, it may work now.

This case, however, was more complicated. The police already had the evidence: the machines and the raw materials. So what did this man want from me? He had said that if I helped him, things would go better for my friends. But what kind of help did they want? They apparently knew that I was close to the boys and the officer wanted me to give them the names of the soldiers who were buying the stuff from them. I denied knowing anything about it. He threatened me with arrest, but for some reason I didn't take him seriously. After some time, he let me go home. I now felt that I had something to work with: I had met the man who literally had my friends' lives in his hands.

I went back to the house and told my girlfriends what had happened in the meeting, but didn't tell them what I was thinking. I hadn't quite crystallized my thoughts yet and only had the beginnings of a plan. A few days later, when I was called in to talk to this man again, I found out that he was in fact the chief of police. His tone was different at our second meeting and he questioned me about matters that really had nothing to do with the case: my age, my background, my family. I began to like this man and to trust him. As I was leaving, he told me that I could see the boys and bring them some food. I hadn't been so happy for a long time. I came home and the girls were also delighted. I packed a big basket of food and went to see the boys – they couldn't believe it when they saw me. They had tears in their eyes. I tried to stay calm and told them that they were going to be okay. I didn't know how, but miracles do happen.

Three weeks had passed since their arrest. I had a plan and was ready to act on it; it was time for me to catch the police chief outside his office. The police station was on one of Kutaisi's main streets – I walked back and forth in front of it for a few days trying to be inconspicuous. Once I saw him walk out, but he wasn't alone. Another time, there was a car waiting for him. I was losing my courage and patience, but I couldn't give up.

Finally the day arrived when I saw him walk out of the station alone. It was already dark and since he was on foot, I thought that he was probably on his way to a nearby restaurant. I started to follow him, but he must have felt my eyes in the back of his head because suddenly he turned around and saw me. I saw him hesitate and then look around to see if anyone else was watching. "Walk a little further," he said to me. "I'll pick you up in my car." This was the moment I'd been waiting for. When the car pulled up beside me I got in and we drove off. He stopped on a rather desolate side street but I wasn't a bit afraid. My instincts told me to trust him.

Once again, my ability to touch people, combined with my innocent little-girl looks, served me well. I spoke to him in much the same way that I had to the NKVD officer in Staliniri, except that this time I was fighting for the lives of four young boys. I talked and talked for quite a long time. I told him about my background in detail and described who the boys were to me. I explained that one of them, Henry, had literally saved my life. I made it all sound very dramatic, but there was really no need for it because the facts spoke for themselves – everything I told him was true. As it turned out, he had young boys himself and, as he admitted later, like most Georgians, he didn't believe much in the Soviet system either. But he still wasn't sure how he could help me without endangering himself.

From that point on, though, I met him before the boys' hearings and, based on what he told me, I was able to coach the boys on what to say. To avoid being discovered, he once called me into his office and he yelled at me in front of some other people. I really had to be an actress and pretend to be upset because his performance made me want to laugh. Finally, at one of our meetings in a safe spot he told me that he had worked out a scheme to get my friends home. He had a very good and trusted friend in one of the smaller police stations and since they were so "overloaded" in the main station, he would just have to transfer the boys' files to him. The chief said that the files would somehow get "lost" in the transfer; it might take years before they reached his friend – if they got there at all. In the meantime, with any luck, the war would come to an end and the boys would go back to Poland. Nobody would ever know anything. I was speechless. I didn't know what to say, so I leaned over and kissed him. He said, "That isn't necessary. As a matter of fact, this whole incident has added some meaning to my life, doing something worthwhile."

I in turn was moved by his words; I knew that he would do what he said, that it was only a question of time before the boys were free. My girlfriends knew that I was trying to help the boys, but I didn't dare tell them any of the details in case something went wrong. I didn't want to build up anybody's hopes. Two or three days after our meeting, the boys came home, straight to our place. Their joy was unreal; I almost felt uncomfortable with their thanks. I told them the whole story and became "queen for the day." People came over to congratulate us and see the boys. I was a sensation in the community.

We had parties for a few days. Henry said that we were even – now I had saved his life. The boys were jumping around me, buying me all kinds of gifts.

The chief had asked me to call him after they got home, which I did. He met me again and told me that they could continue their operation, that he would warn me if information about another impending arrest came to him. He also told me who had betrayed them.

Whenever new people came to town we invited them for dinner and arranged quite elaborate parties to introduce them to the community. The last person who had arrived was a young man who wasn't happy living in a small town somewhere near Kutaisi and was trying to find a way to move to the city. It was this young man who had informed on the boys, which is why the police knew about us girls and the whole operation. What a low creature – we had treated him with such generosity. He had stayed with the boys for a few days and we had given him lots of help. He didn't even deserve the energy it would take to hate him. One can only pity this kind of man. I don't know what happened to him later; we lost all contact with him.

Shortly after the whole thing was over, I was invited to the chief's home for dinner and met his beautiful wife and children. Fortunately there are also decent people in this world, people who made our survival possible.

~

Life continued as it had before. I went over to help the boys with their work, but for some unknown reason, my relationship with the girls suddenly changed. They started picking on me, disagreeing with everything I said. I couldn't believe that they were jealous of me, but that's what it looked like. I felt terrible. Staying with the girls became unbearable – the boys could see it too but they couldn't interfere; it wouldn't have been right. They suggested that I move out and rented a room for me with a Georgian family across the road from their flat. I was devastated by my roommates' behaviour – it was a blow to my ego, to my whole being. I felt a deep loss and was depressed for a long time. What had I done to them? I never asked; I just moved out.

The boys' next-door neighbours were also from Poland, two brothers named Tenenbaum and their brother-in-law who had all escaped together. They had been shoe manufacturers in Poland and had managed to get involved in the same business in Kutiasi on a smaller scale. Since meeting them, I had gotten many beautiful shoes. They had visited us girls very often and the older of the two brothers, Joseph, was a very pleasant, intelligent man, not especially attractive, but fine, reserved, well-mannered and soft-spoken. I knew he liked me but I hadn't paid any attention to him since I was still preoccupied with Levan.

But I had lost Levan and now I had lost the girls. Joseph became my confidante and began to see me alone and take me out in the evenings to the theatre and movies and so on. He was good company – attentive and easy to be with. He was much older than me and had been married before the war and had a little girl. Over time, we became very comfortable with each other. Without realizing it, without any premeditation, we slipped into an intimate relationship.

Being with Joseph was very different from being with Levan. I wasn't in love with him, but I liked him enough to get involved. It was pleasant, enjoyable and satisfying; at this difficult time, I felt that he was my saviour. I needed somebody to take care of me to a certain extent. After so many difficult experiences I was tired and needed a relationship like that – quiet, peaceful, without strings attached, without sparks flying – even though he professed his love for me. He was married, but neither of us felt guilty. We all needed to live for the moment because tomorrow was unknown. Joseph provided me with an emotional shelter that was safe and secure without making any demands. He gave his unconditional friendship and for that I was thankful; I considered myself very fortunate. I shall always remember him as one of the most sincere, honest people I have ever known. We needed each other in different ways, with mutual respect and understanding. As I had already found out, there are indeed many kinds of relationships.

Nobody had ever told me how to behave in relationships. I followed my own ideas and always tried, no matter what, to be honest and open with the other person. I couldn't have survived mentally if I hadn't preserved my integrity and followed some very strict principles I set for myself. As a result, I never lost my self-respect or the respect of others, and never ended a relationship on bad terms. The people I allowed to enter my life contributed a lot to my well-being and growth. There can be mutual giving under so many different circumstances.

The days were passing by in my new environment and I was comfortable and quite secure with the boys around me, including Joseph. We knew that the war was coming to an end and that the Germans were being defeated – the Allied victory was only a matter of time. The Germans were being chased on all fronts. We were able to follow the news since the Soviets, as the great victors, were now giving the people full reports.

I don't know how many thousands of people like us were scattered all over the Soviet Union, but we knew that we would all be allowed to go back home when the war was over. We just didn't know when and how that would happen. Here, again, I was lucky. My friend the chief of police sent a note asking me to come and see him. He told me that since the Soviets were already close to the Polish border, it was time for me to make preparations for my departure. He said that the journey back to Poland would be long and difficult since the effects of the war were still being felt everywhere, I was better off starting early. Listening to him, I couldn't control myself and started crying. I was so grateful to this man and there was nothing I could do in return. He repeated what he had told me once before. "You gave me the opportunity to do something worthwhile in my life and I thank you for it," he said. "In my type of work a lot of people hate me and I don't blame them. I hate my position, but in this system, you do what you are told to do. You can't just quit and do what you like." Everything became clearer to me and I felt sorry for him and his family. He asked me how many transit passes I needed, with limits, of course. At that point, he didn't specify how many he would be able to give me or how he would get them. I didn't ask.

Now I had a new dilemma: if I asked for too many passes, he might think that I was asking too much of him. I decided to be honest. I told him that I needed four for the boys, three for the Tenenbaums and one for me. What about the girls? I had to include them too and so I asked for eleven passes, exactly what I felt was fair. He agreed. This was the beginning of 1945.

It took a few weeks for me to receive the passes. The boys took the ones for the girls over to them. I told them not to mention that they were getting the passes thanks to me. We started to liquidate whatever we had in Kutaisi and got ready to travel. I was now entering a new phase of my war experiences – the big journey back. Fear automatically set in. What would I find there? I tried to prepare myself emotionally for my homecoming, but I couldn't visualize anything, so I let it go and pushed my fears away. We didn't talk about it amongst ourselves either. We didn't know anything about what had happened in Europe during the war.

I decided to write a goodbye letter to Levan. We didn't tell anybody in our community about our leaving so early, which was only common sense. We also decided not to travel as a group. In the chaotic conditions that existed during and after a war, it was difficult to know when or how we would find enough space on a train to even stand alone; trying to travel together in a group would be impossible. Naturally, I decided to travel with Joseph. The last few weeks I was very busy and, strangely, felt sad again to be leaving yet another place. I would be facing another new beginning and, as usual, I was questioning what was ahead of me.

A few days before I left, early in the morning, a little neighbourhood boy handed me a note. When I opened it, I saw to my great disbelief that it was from Levan – he was standing at the corner of my street. He had come to say goodbye and was afraid that if he had asked my permission I would have refused, so he wasn't taking any chances. My first reaction was great excitement, followed by confusion. Part of me wished that he would leave me alone at this point in my life. I had so much to deal with. Now that he was here, what was I to do? I had to see him. So I walked over to the corner and there he was. We didn't jump at each other, but instead shook hands, standing in silence for a couple of minutes. Neither of us wanted to say too much. We met in the evening for dinner and talked for three hours. He wanted to know every detail of my life in Kutaisi and told me about himself. At the end of the evening, I went back home and he stayed with some friends in town.

We met again the next evening. He asked me if there was any hope that I would keep in touch with him and leave open the possibility of continuing our relationship. I had to be honest with him – no matter what I found at home, I would never be able to live in the Soviet Union. Since there was no hope at all that he could leave, I told him, we were better off not building false hopes. He understood. He walked me to the corner of my street and we said our final goodbyes. We never saw each other again.

The time for our departure was getting closer and we decided to set out in twos or threes a few days apart. Joseph and I were to leave first. We didn't even know where in Poland we would meet the rest of our group, but we knew that somewhere, somehow, sometime, we would see each other again.

Encountering the Truth

I packed a knapsack, as I had on my journey out of Poland, but now I was on my way back. This time, though, my knapsack was larger and nicer. I also took a suitcase small enough to drag along with me since I had some nice clothes that were precious cargo. I was lucky to be travelling with Joseph – in times of hardship, it is nice to have a good companion and he was good to me.

By this time it was late March 1945 and spring was approaching. The trip wasn't as bad as we had anticipated; maybe it was because I was getting used to all kinds of adventures. This time we at least had enough money to buy food, no matter how expensive it was. This hadn't been the case when I was travelling south to Georgia from Arkhangelsk. Now, although we slept on railway station benches, we had some blankets with us to make them a little softer, and to our great surprise we were always able to find seats on the trains. We even managed to stop a few times in small towns and find a local public bathhouse to wash up. The only terrible encounters we had were with groups of men who had left labour camps and were also trying to get back to Poland. They were like walking ghosts, human skeletons. Big, staring eyes, tautly drawn skin, faces full of fear. We tried to talk to them and they barely answered; they only mumbled in Polish or Yiddish.

At first, I couldn't understand why those people hadn't been taken care of, as my group had been. We asked them where they had been and eventually pieced together the information that they had been sent to extremely hard labour camps, where very few had survived. I had been lucky to be in Arkhangelsk. We also saw some Soviet citizens who had survived labour camps, but we couldn't understand them very well. They all seemed too dazed and bewildered to communicate; we couldn't figure out why they had been freed or where they were going. The sight of them remained engraved in my memory for a long time.

After six weeks or so of travelling we reached the city of Lvov, which had been Polish before the war. When the Soviets and Germans divided Poland in 1939, Lvov had become part of the Soviet Union. I had never been there before, although Lvov was one of the Polish cities with the most culture and historic architectural sites. It was there that we heard the big news on May 15, 1945: the Germans had surrendered. Naturally, the response to the news was great – masses of people were out in the streets shouting and singing patriotic songs. According to Soviet custom, the loudspeakers thundered with music all over the city.

I found the victory bittersweet. I am sure that there was hardly a person who hadn't paid a price in this war. I for one couldn't take part in all the excitement. My mind was elsewhere, as was Joseph's. We hardly talked – the tension hung in the air and we didn't dare to touch the untouchable subject of our families. As we got closer to our destination – Lodz – I became more and more afraid. I felt like running away again, but where would I go?

We came across some Jewish people and started hearing rumours about what had happened to the Jews during the war, but I wasn't yet prepared to listen to what they were saying. I closed my mind. I tried to postpone the encounter as long as possible. For the rest of the trip, the few days it took to reach Lodz, the two of us were very quiet, each buried under the weight of our inner fears, almost embarrassed to face each other so as not to show the agony we felt. My thoughts were so mixed up, jumping from one member of my family to the next. The years I had spent away had been completely erased. All I could think was, what if? Suddenly, I didn't want to go home. If only I could use some magic trick and disappear, or become somebody else. I was torturing myself to the point that Joseph later told me that he thought I had lost my mind.

When we finally arrived in Lodz, I was so mentally exhausted that I really was afraid that I was having a breakdown. "I can't do it now, but I went through so much, how can I give in now? I must stop this; I must go on." I kept talking to myself and poor Joseph didn't know what to do with me. Somehow I got a hold of myself – after all, I was a survivor.

Lodz had been liberated some time ago – it had taken the Red Army a few months to march from there to Berlin – so we did encounter some Jewish survivors in the streets, a group of young people who looked so normal compared to those we had seen on the train. We couldn't figure them out at all. We told them we had come back from the Soviet Union and asked if they would tell us where to go, what to do. They gave us all the necessary directions as to where to go first – to the Jewish Committee, where we could get assistance in various social services. We walked into a room in a building located on a main street of Lodz, which was buzzing with people and had lists posted on the walls. There was a whole army of people to help us, speaking almost every language, but I looked around and felt like a trapped animal. This was it. This was the end of the road. I understood that the fate of my family was posted on the long lists that covered all the walls. The Jewish Committee had made the task of searching easier by listing only the names of survivors.

At this point, we still didn't know anything. I walked away from Joseph. I didn't want him to be near me when I learned about my family. I needed to pull together all the inner strength I had and force myself to walk toward the lists, to look under the letter K. I was shaking. I didn't see anybody around me. I was all alone, alone with my pain. My eyes moved down the list of Ks. I stopped at the end, closed my eyes for a minute and started all over again. Maybe I had missed our name…. The letters became very hazy. My head was spinning. Neither of my parents nor any of my brothers' names were there – could it be that they didn't have all the survivors' names yet? It's only the beginning, I told myself. They might still show up. Somebody had to have survived. My two parents. My four brothers. In my great shock, I forgot that my sister's name wasn't Kohn – her husband's name was Laziczak. I quickly looked under L. There she was! She was alive! I was overjoyed to see that she had survived, but what about the rest? Was she the only survivor? I looked at Joseph, pale and shaken. He leaned against the wall and announced in a faint voice, "No one from my people is on the wall."

Many years later, when I visited Israel and stood at the Wailing Wall in Jerusalem, I was struck by the memory that I had been at a wailing wall once before – the wall covered with the long lists of only survivors.

Joseph took my arm. "Let's go," he said firmly. We walked out of the building, dragging our feet slowly, not really knowing where to go. Our feet seemed to take over and our minds disconnected from them: left foot, right foot, on and on aimlessly. We were oblivious to our surroundings and hadn't yet absorbed where we were. This was Lodz, a city where I had so many memories from before the war.

Suddenly I stopped. I recognized the building where my aunt and her family had lived, the relatives I had delivered bread to at the beginning of the war. The shock of it brought me back to reality and I said to Joseph, "Enough! Where are we going? We have to look for people we know – we didn't even look at the list of survivors from my town – relatives or friends. Let's go back."

I quickly ran through the names of some of my friends. I saw quite a few, but the one I stopped at was Sztainhorn. The two sisters of Henry and Abraham, two of my "four boys" – one of them was my schoolmate Bela. Joseph found some names from his hometown who were also in Lodz now. I took down the address of the two girls and that was my first destination – 33 Piotrkowska Street, a very central, main street in Lodz. I said goodbye to Joseph. He knew where to reach me.

The courtyard was typical of Lodz – a big passageway in front surrounded by four-storey buildings with large apartments and at the back a passageway leading to another similar courtyard with an entrance to the next block on another street named Danska. I found the apartment of the two sisters on the second floor of the building. I rang the bell and a short, sweet, nicely dressed dark-haired girl with buck teeth opened the door. I was tongue-tied for a moment – after all, it had been eight years since I had left school and Bela's sister, Rose, was two years younger than me. I didn't really know her. Finally, I said, "I hope I have the right place. I am Basia Kohn." She threw herself at me and talked for a solid minute about how she had lived very close to my family in the ghetto. I couldn't listen to what she was saying and wished she would stop; I was afraid that she would tell me too much too soon. All I wanted was to tell her about her two brothers, how close I had been to them in the Soviet Union and that they were on their way home, that they should arrive in a matter of days. While I was standing there in the hallway Bela came in and we recognized each other immediately. Our greeting turned into a big cry, which I needed so badly.

She looked gorgeous, more beautiful than I remembered. She was my height, five foot two, and very slim, with big grey eyes and dark hair. She took over and said right away, "Basia, this is your home as long you need it." I told her briefly about her two brothers, which made our reunion even more dramatic. I looked around and saw a beautifully furnished four-room flat with rooms that were much larger than the average apartment in Canada.

The two sisters had been liberated very early from a camp in Germany by the Soviet army before the end of the war and had made their way back to Poland. On the way, Bela had met a Polish army officer, a Jewish man named Ben Herzog, who took an interest in her and helped the two sisters get settled. Being an army officer with the Polish armed forces, he had no problem getting an apartment that had been occupied by Germans who had fled with the retreating army. They had left everything behind, even clothes. Many war survivors in Lodz lived in these nice apartments abandoned by the Germans.

I began to understand a little more about the war as time went on, but right then I was completely disconnected. I told Bela that I needed a little rest before anything, before my re-entry into the country of my birth, the country where I spent the first sixteen years of my life. It turned out to be a strange new place; I might just as well have been dropped onto another planet, except for the language. Socially, economically and politically, it was a new post-war era. I knew that I would have to tread very slowly and carefully. There was so much to deal with. I needed to allow myself time to absorb this new world – people who were supposedly old friends weren't the same anymore. The most nagging questions I had, I didn't dare to ask yet. Afraid of the answers, I had to wait. Bela helped me unpack and hang up my clothes. She prepared a bath for me – a luxury I couldn't even remember – and I went to sleep. I apologized for my behaviour, but she understood.

The next morning, I woke up and looked around. I was in a double bed in a beautifully furnished bedroom. I thought that I was dreaming. Bela and Rose came in when they heard me and I started crying. They treated me like a sick child. A typical pre-war breakfast was waiting for me on the table in the dining room. I had no idea where they had gotten the food. In fact, all the Jewish survivors were getting a lot of help from the Jewish Committees that had been set up everywhere. Bela's army officer friend, Ben Herzog, had also been able to get them lots of things thanks to his new high position in the Polish provisional government. He married Bela shortly afterwards.

For the first few days, I stayed in almost complete isolation with the two girls. Rose was the cook and she prepared beautiful meals.

I don't know where she had learned how to do it. They had already been in Lodz for two or three months. Finally, we started talking. My first bits of information came from them, to be filled in by many more people in the weeks and months to come. They had started off in the ghetto in Zduńska Wola and then everyone, including my family, had been shipped to the ghetto in Lodz in August 1942. They told me about the liquidation of the Lodz ghetto in August 1944, the segregation of the old, the sick and the very young, how they were shipped to the unknown – to what everyone later learned were the Auschwitz gas chambers. The physically capable ones had been sent off to work at labour camps under subhuman conditions.

I couldn't get over the way they were able to tell me about the heartbreaking horrors they experienced in the most calm, matter-of-fact tone. They told me how their family – their older sister, younger brother and father (their mother had died when they were very small) – had perished along with a great number of relatives and friends. This was my first encounter with the word Holocaust. After the war, the whole world, not only I, had to face it, a word that has weighed and will continue to weigh heavily on the consciousness of nations and individuals alike forever. The guilt cannot be limited to one man or one nation – mankind stands accused for not helping and not preventing it when there was still time.

I couldn't cry anymore. Tears alone weren't enough. Now I wanted to know as much as possible about what had happened to European Jews, every detail. Even though I couldn't face knowing more about what had happened to my family, I couldn't spare myself now. My pain grew with every new piece of information, but I had to know everything. Paradoxically, the more I hurt, the better I felt. Somebody told me that as early as 1942 a group of Jewish women from Poland had arrived in Palestine and brought shattering reports of the systematic decimation of European Jewry. So the rest of the world knew about it. Nobody helped our people, who have been treated so unjustly and abused so miserably throughout history. I heard how people witnessed the world around them being virtually destroyed, thousands of people perishing daily. How should we grieve for them, for their suffering and their pain?

After a few days, the two Sztainhorn brothers arrived. As I had, they saw the names of their two sisters on the list and their joy was indescribable. I removed myself for a while and let the four Sztainhorns have their turn and go through the inevitable.

There was so much to understand, absorb and learn. I wondered how my life would now unfold. If I could only know what was ahead of me. I was so tired of the unexpected and unknown. I kept thinking that nature seemed to have some perverse quirks, insisting on suffering as a prerequisite to growth. Is it really necessary? I questioned everything without getting any answers. As usual, though, I had to go on. We were the remnants of an era that will fill history books for generations to come – we were the survivors. Once again, I had to deal with a new environment and once again I was a stranger, even in my own country. But I was finally ready to venture out and face the world around me.

I started looking up all my friends who were in Lodz. A whole group of my school friends were living in one large apartment not far from where I was staying. Our meeting was very strange because I had come from such a different world than they had and we were all much older now. We had been fourteen when we parted ways and it was now eight years later; we weren't little girls and boys anymore; we were now young women and men. This particular group consisted of all the well-off kids; the girls were even prettier now than they had been before the war and the boys were all better-looking too. But the most interesting and disturbing observation I had was that they all behaved so normally: they were well-dressed and in very good spirits. Joking, laughing. It seemed to me, in the weeks to come, that whenever I visited them there was a continuous party going on, as though they didn't want to remember anything and were trying to get the most out of every minute.

I also could see that the interactions between the sexes were very free and unrestrained, something we hadn't experienced in my world. They accepted me very warmly, but I felt that I didn't fit in. I came with different baggage. I could understand the way that most of the young people were behaving, but I couldn't be part of it. Another phenomenon of this period was that people were getting married left and right. They were mostly young people – I think that very few were over forty years old – but the mismatches were unbelievable to me. I saw some of my school girlfriends, young women from nice families, marrying men who were much older and below their intellectual level as long as they had money.

We were all in the same situation now but we had arrived there via different experiences. Theirs had been one long horror story; mine was a chain of events that, although not rosy, was still incomparable to theirs. As I write this, I know that I have a different perspective on life. I feel that I was enriched through my sometimes dramatic and difficult times. I still feel whole. I am still together. People who were directly victimized by Nazi policies to murder Jews during the Holocaust have scars that might never heal. Acknowledging these realities made me want to try to understand their behaviour.

I heard plenty of information from my friends in Lodz; everyone slowly filled me in. I knew by now there was no one else to wait for. I had to learn to live with it, like all the people around me. There was one difference between their acceptance and mine – because they had been in the midst of the horror, they had been slowly prepared for it – in some way, their very survival obscured the immediate pain of loss. I lived those years expecting bad news, but in my wildest nightmares I couldn't possibly have imagined the premeditated destruction of human life by other human beings. This new knowledge was too wounding, too burning, so enormously devastating.

I knew that I needed time to come to terms with this knowledge. I became very introspective, reflecting on my life. I recall hearing somewhere that to be brave one has to be lonely. I wonder if it's true. During this chaotic time, I lived in a world that was sometimes of my own making and at other times I felt that I was just being thrown around. Most of the time I felt like a drop of oil on water, sometimes afloat, sometimes submerged, but always separate, never merging with another drop. My life felt so out of control, as it had so many times before, and with the lack of control came the all-too-familiar fears: fears of feeling helpless, stranded, abandoned. How does one integrate one's own individual past and present, especially when the present becomes past so quickly and drastically? How does one adapt to so many total changes? One does, but one pays a tremendous price.

~

After a couple of weeks, I got in touch with my sister, who had survived the war in a series of labour camps, working in armaments factories. Her letters were very odd. I don't want to use another word because at that point there were so many encounters I couldn't comprehend. I also got in touch with my brother in Israel, but he was a stranger to me – he had left for Palestine when I was only six or seven years old. My sister had intended to go to Palestine after the war, but she now found herself in Marburg in the American-occupied zone of Germany. Many survivors like her were waiting to emigrate somewhere, to relatives in the United States, Canada, South America or Palestine. Meanwhile they lived very well in the American Zone and were heavily involved in different kinds of black marketeering and, eventually, legitimate businesses. I later heard that some of them made a lot of money. My sister didn't go into details about our family in her letters. All she told me was that she knew how everyone had perished, that she would give me the morbid details when we met. She never did – and I never wanted to know.

After the Stzainhorn brothers came to themselves, we all settled into a family unit. There were the two brothers, Rose, Bela and me. After a few weeks of mourning, Henry and Abraham began to think in practical terms about making a living. Naturally they turned to what they knew best, manufacturing sewing threads.

Poland had been under Communist influence since early 1945. The process of nationalization had begun, but there were still small private enterprises of up to about fifty employees. Individuals didn't yet feel the Communist Party's power and oppression since the official Communist rule of Poland had not yet begun. So, on the streets of Lodz, life seemed very normal. Stores were open and full of merchandise and there was plenty of food, although everything was very expensive. All the survivors I came in contact with seemed to live very well. It was puzzling to me how it was possible in such a short time. They were involved in all kinds of businesses and some of them were fairly shady, like deals with Soviet soldiers who were smuggling goods back to the USSR.

Henry and Abraham rented a place, bought the machines they needed for their operation and made contacts. In no time, they were back in business. I worked with them again, running the office and dealing with storekeepers and other clients. Our place, just as it had in Kutaisi, became a meeting place for everyone. Rose stayed home and she took care of the household by shopping and cooking. We had company for dinner and every day was like a party. Srulek and Aaron came back and stayed with us for a few days and then took off to Germany, to the American Zone. A lot of people were planning to go there since the borders were very easy to cross right after the war and one could get all the assistance one needed to emigrate.

Hela, her sister, Lola, and Feiga also came to Lodz and their first stop was our place. Our greeting was quite friendly – not too effusive, but I was satisfied with it. They thanked me for getting them the passes; the boys had eventually told them how they had gotten them. We helped them find a place to live, but they were on their own. They sometimes came to visit us, but although we maintained a friendly relationship we lived in different worlds.

I heard from Joseph Tenenbaum a few times too. As we had agreed, we remained friends. He didn't want to interfere with my life and I wouldn't have wanted him to. Something very beautiful and dramatic happened to him. Quite late, since not all the names of the survivors had been listed in the beginning, he found out that his wife and daughter were alive in the American Zone in Germany. He came to tell me the good news and to say goodbye as he was leaving to join them there. I was very happy for him; I heard later that they ended up in Israel, but his younger brother unfortunately died shortly after their arrival there.

I tried to keep track of most of the people I encountered during the war as much as possible. It was interesting to see how they spread out all over the world. Shortly after coming to Lodz, Feiga left for Sweden because some friends of her parents were living there. Srulek went to Israel, where he had two sisters who had immigrated before the war. His family in Poland had also been obliterated.

Meanwhile, Bela's boyfriend, Ben Herzog, arrived on the scene, a man of thirty-five or thirty-six. He was quite pleasant-looking, so-phisticated, charming and suave – very much a gentleman. Before the war he had worked in his parents' ocean-liner shipping business. He was a very assimilated Jew and didn't even understand Yiddish. He took Bela with him to Bucharest, Romania, where he had been trans-ferred in some diplomatic capacity. She moved into a new exciting world, although it later turned out that he was quite unfaithful to her. She visited a few times, dressed in the most fashionable clothes, just a stunning girl. A year or two later they immigrated to Brazil, where her husband had a very rich uncle.

Another interesting event during this first year was the arrival of Yanka from the Soviet Union. She was a nurse and was living with her boyfriend. People from the Soviet Union came at different intervals – some didn't arrive until two or three years after the war. Some had been kept in prisons longer, some in labour camps; some of them looked even worse than the Holocaust survivors. I really liked Yanka and was glad when she rented an apartment with her boyfriend not far from ours and settled down to family life. Unfortunately, it wasn't long before his wife appeared on the scene. I don't know where she had been, but the most bizarre triangle emerged. Yanka's boyfriend, naturally excited about seeing his wife, took her into the apartment and into the bed he shared with Yanka. My girlfriend readily accepted the part of his new-found cousin and slept on the couch in the living room.

I was shocked. I still can't understand how and why she could possibly do such a thing. What were her motives? I don't know whether she knew herself and I don't know whether her behaviour should be admired or judged. But in that post-war era, the most unusual situations were taking place everywhere. There were no precedents to go by; one just had to play one's part unrehearsed, improvising. As time went on, Yanka felt the need to talk to someone and we became very close. She spent a lot of time at our place. She finally decided that she couldn't take the situation anymore and moved out, not knowing what to do or where to go.

Around this time, I ran into Moniek Reichman, a dentist from Częstochowa. He and his two younger brothers had been in the same labour camp as me in Arkhangelsk. He was about twelve or more years older than me, a tall, nice-looking man who made a very comfortable living working as a dentist. That was all I knew about him. We began to see each other; he often came over for dinners or parties, took me to the many theatres in Lodz, and I also visited his place. But either something was missing or I just wasn't capable of receiving or giving. Not at this time perhaps, not yet. But we continued to see each other. He was an ardent Zionist and was involved in the Bricha movement to help people leave Poland to get to Italy and from there to pre-state Israel. At that time, the British wouldn't allow any survivors into Palestine; they kept them isolated on the island of Cyprus for a long time. As a matter of fact, one of the four boys, Aaron, drowned while trying to reach the banks of Haifa. He was only twenty-three years old. What a tragedy, to have survived the war, only to lose his life because of British restrictions against Jews.

During this first year in Lodz, I met a number of men who were older than me. Yanka introduced me to a man she knew from Lvov who had been a lawyer before the war and was now a state prosecutor. But I still couldn't connect with anyone. Part of it was also that I still remembered my intense affair with Levan – everything else seemed like just a casual relationship. The excitement wasn't there; I just wasn't ready for any commitment to anyone. My war years hadn't exactly been normal and the present was so unreal and so temporary that I felt very detached. This was true even though I never slept alone – I always had some girlfriends or friends around me.

We, the girls, went through a complete makeover in a short time. We dressed well, very much in style. At that time, short skirts and long jackets were in and so were hats, hats with everything – with suits, coats and even with dresses. But the most dramatic change was that I started using makeup, which I had never used before.

I was twenty-three years old. My feelings about myself as a woman were very mixed up because I had missed any kind of normal teenage period. I felt so childish in some ways, yet I was dressed up and made up like a woman. These represented two very conflicting images of myself. But I followed the crowd and being fashionable was the trend among my contemporaries.

David

One very memorable day in the summer of 1946, David and his roommates arrived. I will never forget the look on his face when he saw me. I couldn't understand it at the time, but I realized later it was because, although he looked just the same to me, I had changed quite a bit. Within a year I had become a woman trying to look sophisticated with a heavily made-up face, tweezed narrow eyebrows and dark, heavy lipstick. He remembered the little girl I had been when I last saw him. He came over for dinner and was very quiet, looking at me differently. I didn't pay much attention to him; I was still involved with Moniek and, in general, I was attracted to older, more experienced men.

He came to our place very often. Rose liked him immediately, but the poor girl was so put down by her sister, Bela, that she had no confidence in herself at all. David, being polite, paid attention to her as the hostess and I was afraid that she would take him seriously. I knew David well enough to know that he wouldn't be interested in her.

I became very close to Rose, more so than to her sister. I really helped her build up her confidence and literally took over her education. We found a teacher to give her private tutoring. Next, I took her to a dentist and helped her go through a series of operations to correct her teeth. Some were taken out and some were put back – it was a very new technique. She was thankful to me for the rest of her life because it completely changed her looks and affected her whole personality. I think she was the nicest, most honest, good-natured person I have ever met. She was sensitive to others and very intelligent. I kept up my friendship with her for a very long time and last met up with her in Israel in 1973.

David settled in Lodz and went into the same business as the Sztainhorn brothers. They didn't mind; there was room for everyone. His two roommates left Poland for the western zones of occupied Germany in order to immigrate to Palestine. So David was left alone, waiting to go to Canada. His father had left most of the family – his mother, sister, younger brother and David – behind in Poland in 1936 to immigrate to Canada because he had three sisters there. He had money and was allowed into the country as a businessman. He had taken his eldest son, Jack, with him, but David had heard from his relatives that his brother was no damn good at all to his father. David's father had settled in some kind of business in Canada and intended to bring the family over. In the meantime, though, the war broke out and, to his great horror, his family was stranded in Poland. David got in touch with his brother after the war and received the sad news that his father had died just the year before. The guilt of leaving the family behind and finding out what had happened to them had literally killed him. He got sick and never recovered. He died at the age of forty-four.

David was devastated by the news and I felt really sorry for him. He had moved into a hotel room for the time being and wasn't very happy about it. I spent more time talking to him but still didn't treat him as a possible boyfriend. He was only one year older than me. He saw different men taking me out and what he felt or thought, I didn't know. All my school girlfriends who met him liked him a lot, but he kept pretty much to himself, passing the time until he could join his brother in Canada.

Meanwhile, the older Sztainhorn brother, Henry, fell in love with a girl who was very unsuitable for him. It was such a pity to watch a marriage that was doomed from the start. She thought he had money and he thought he could change her with his love. She was beautiful but very ordinary and no match for him at all. They took over the bedroom where Rose and I slept so I decided to move out and get a place with Yanka. We took one room in an apartment that belonged to a woman named Cesia, the daughter of a former surgeon in Warsaw, Dr. Soloweijczyk. Her husband had been an army officer and she had a beautiful, modern five-room apartment. Unfortunately, with the growing shortage of living space in Lodz, she had to give up all but one room. The kitchen was for mutual use. So the two of us settled into another routine, a new social life. We took some vacations together and on one of them Yanka met a young man, an engineer from France. She kept up a correspondence with him for some time.

A lot of my friends were leaving in search of a better life and eventually very few remained in Poland – just a few Jews who had been communists before the war and hadn't yet had the chance to become disillusioned with communist ideals. All this made me wonder why I didn't have any plans.

David moved out of the hotel and got a room with the Kruk family, a Jewish lawyer and his Polish wife who had helped him during the war. She had actually risked her own life and the lives of her relatives to hide him. Shortly after David moved in with them, there was an influenza outbreak and many people died. I had it but somehow managed to pull through. David got it very badly and Yanka, being a nurse, looked after him. While he was recovering, I used to go to his room and spend time with him. I really began to respond more to him – although it was still strictly as a friend. At the same time, Moniek finished his Zionist mission in Poland and got instructions from his organization to leave immediately. The work he was doing was very much underground. I wasn't in love with him, but his leaving left a void just the same.

So David and I began a strange almost child-like relationship. David wasn't at all experienced and, as I've said, he was only a year older than me. By now I had had a few involvements with men who were quite a bit older than me. But I just allowed things to take their course. I didn't premeditate anything, I didn't know where it was going, but I could be myself with him and let him be himself. We drew closer and began to spend more time together, quite often with Yanka as well. I didn't want to leave her by herself. I was still very naive in certain ways and I felt that I needed her. Being four or five years older, she had a big affect on me.

David was very shy. It took him ages to even kiss me, but there was something in him that was pure, honest and strong. I started thinking about him differently. Maybe, after all, what I had said all those years ago would come true – that if worse comes to worst, when I came back to Poland, I could always marry David and go with him to Canada.

As I have said many times, I believe in fate. Events have a habit of going a certain way, no matter how much you think you direct and control them. David and I began to link our futures together, very cautiously at first since we both knew how different we were and how many adjustments we would each have to make. There wasn't any I-can't-live-without-you talk. The word love didn't even come up and neither of us was very demonstrative. In a way, it was a mature, rather pragmatic approach, and yet I think that he had a lot of feelings for me. The biggest obstacle for me was that I thought he was too young. I didn't let it stop me though. Something inside was telling me to give the two of us a chance. I'm sure that he had some trepidations as well. He told me that he had barely recognized me when he first arrived and he didn't like what he saw. I knew it – I told him that I could see it in his eyes. We decided to go forward and find out if we could work out the differences in some of our outlooks and attitudes. Our physical interaction was very different from anything I had experienced before. At the time, I blamed it all on the fact that, having had some relationships, I was more experienced than he was and that maybe he was nervous.

We became accustomed to each other as two independent people. I was self-sufficient financially and so was he. Not that I had any money saved – I spent everything I made with the Sztainhorns. I didn't take money seriously. I lived for today, the same as I do now. The difference was I lived much better. But I still had the same feeling of being suspended in the air, of waiting for another change.

While I was living with Yanka, I made quite a few interesting friends that I shared with David. In our apartment were the landlady, Cesia, and her husband, and Ruth, the former wife of a Jewish comedian who had been well-known before the war, and her new husband, a well-to-do jeweller. They were friends of Yanka's from Lvov. We were also friendly with David's landlord, the Jewish lawyer and his Polish wife. In 1973, I met the lawyer's ex-wife in Israel – she had divorced her husband, left him in Poland and married another Jewish man, a doctor. They were living happily in Tel Aviv.

So we had a nice small social circle that included the Sztainhorns and some of my school girlfriends. We used to entertain each other, go away to resort areas for weekends and go to the theatre and movies. I kept company with David for nearly a year and some of my girlfriends couldn't understand why I was hesitating. They thought that I should be in ecstasy with a boy like David. To them, he represented something unattainable. This is the impression he made on everybody. I didn't even know what to say to them, so I kept quiet. As a matter of fact, Cesia, I guess in a fit of jealousy or exasperation, said to me in front of David and Yanka, "Hair will grow on the palm of my hand if David marries you." I didn't respond. I didn't know what to say and she wouldn't have believed me anyway.

David and I finally had a long, long talk one day. It wasn't anything like the kind of marriage proposal with an engagement ring that I later encountered in Canada. Even today, that seems like prehistoric behaviour to me. Why does the man ask the woman to marry him and why does she wait for the ring? Worse yet, why did they have to ask the parents' permission, specifically asking the father for the hand of his daughter? This is almost comical to me, but I guess that I was ahead of my time.

We considered moving in together for a trial period, but David didn't want that. Even more strange to me was the fact that he insisted on us not being intimate until we got married. He knew that I wasn't a virgin – I had told him all about my affair with Levan, hoping that he would reveal something as well, but I heard nothing. I even told him that I was too young to get married – I was only twenty-three. In my mind, I felt that anyone getting married should really be ready for that great commitment and should take it seriously, for better or worse. Although people were getting married right and left, for me, it was a very big step. I was afraid of the commitment for reasons that I didn't – and still don't – completely understand, so it's no wonder I hesitated for so long.

Despite all this, we set a date at the end of March 1947 for our wedding. We planned to get married before a justice of the peace and then invite some friends to a dinner party. Yanka and the Sztainhorns took care of all the details. As our wedding day approached, we also planned our honeymoon in Kudowa-Zdrój, previously called Bad Kudowa, a very fashionable resort where Hitler used to vacation before the war. After the war, Poland was given territory in the west that had been German before, including this area; at the same time, Poland lost some territory in the east to the Soviet Union.

At that time, we were in an upper-income bracket. Anybody in any private enterprise lived well above both the working people and most professionals. We even had a maid, which David had suggested since Yanka and I were working a lot. She stayed in a small room next to the kitchen and kept the kitchen, washroom and other common areas clean. We didn't have to pay a lot for help – only food was expensive. As it turned out she stole food from us to feed the rest of her family, but we didn't mind.

I even had my clothes made by a French designer. I could never have dreamed about coming even close to this lifestyle before the war.

This was the unreal part of my short period in Poland after the war – I found myself on top without any previous preparation. I knew it was temporary, but I made the most of it. The future was, again, so unknown – we couldn't think about it, let alone worry about it or prepare for it. It was a transition period, so what difference did it make where the money went?

David also had his suits and coats made by a custom tailor. People said that we both made a very nice couple, but I still found myself quite sad during the last few days before the wedding. We wouldn't have one relative with us. Suddenly, I had to go to Zduńska Wola, to at least visit the place where I had last seen my family. I couldn't go to a cemetery, which is what one would normally do, so Zduńska Wola was the closest thing to being able to visit their graves. David went with me.

We rented a car – David knew how to drive since he had driven a truck in Tashkent – and when we got to Zduńska Wola, the town of my birth, I looked around the familiar streets. I could almost see myself walking along the main street, Piłsudski Street, with all my young friends. That had been our great entertainment, walking up and down the main street and meeting friends. I saw the same stores, but they looked different now and had new owners. I remembered the old ones very vividly. Although the memories were mixed with so much pain, suddenly I could only remember the good things. I went to the park, my favourite spot, and it looked the same. Part of me is still there, skating on the ponds in the winter and canoeing in the summer. I had managed to have some beautiful moments even then. We kept driving; like so many times in similar circumstances, I had to have total silence.

I looked at the Polish people, young and old, and my pain very quickly returned. I knew only too well what part they had played in this hideous crime. I was convinced that they could have done it just as well on their own. I wanted to leave right away because I didn't want to have any encounters with local Polish people in case I recognized some of them and said something. I know myself too well.

But I had to go to the street where my house had been, where I had spent the last dreadful few months before embarking on my big journey into the unknown as a scared little girl. We drove into the street where there had been only Jews when I left – now there wasn't a single Jew in sight. As we reached the building where I had lived, I got more and more afraid of what my reaction to the sight of it would be, but I wouldn't give up. I looked at my old house from the car; I couldn't bring myself to get out and walk to the backyard behind the building. I felt as if my legs were paralyzed. I sat there motionless for a few minutes and then burst out crying. I lost control. David held me and didn't say anything.

I never did go into the house. I was afraid to see our furniture still there, with strange people sleeping in my bed. This was my final goodbye to my family, to my sixteen years there, to my relatives, my friends, my dreams and hopes. They were all buried there. The whole town had become one big cemetery to me.

I was glad to leave; it was a ghost town now. I knew now that I would be only too happy to leave Poland forever, to never see it again. I got control of myself and thought about how I was entering yet another new phase in my life. I was binding my whole being to someone new, someone to whom I was willing to surrender unconditionally and expecting the same in return. Maybe that was childish and naive, but those were my true thoughts at the time.

David asked me to also accompany him to his old place in Lodz and his behaviour was very similar to mine, although I didn't know what was going on in his mind. With this behind us, we could go on with our wedding plans.

I still have the photo from the place where we had our wedding dinner party. We had big, beautiful flower arrangements that our friends had sent to us. I was wearing a very simple black dress with elaborate silver embroidery on one arm and on one side at the waist. I wore this dress in Canada after we arrived and everybody admired it.

This is the one and only picture of our wedding I have, and I have to use it in order to refresh my own memory of it. I am surprised myself to see the beautifully set table. Seated first was Cesia, my landlady, and her husband; next to them were the people who occupied another room in the apartment, the ex-wife of the comedian and her husband; then David and me. Next to me was David's landlady, Helen, and her husband and beside them were Ruth and her husband. Standing behind David and me were Rose Sztainhorn, her brother Abraham, Yanka, and Henry Sztainhorn with his wife, Bronka, and our housekeeper.

After dinner, at about ten or eleven o'clock, the group escorted us to the train station, where we took a sleeper to Kudowa-Zdrój – that's where we spent our first night. We stayed in a very elegant hotel where we met a Jewish couple from Warsaw and a Polish couple from Lodz who we often spent time with. We were there for two weeks.

We came back from our honeymoon in the middle of April 1947. We had made an arrangement with Yanka for her to take over David's room at the Kruks' and David moved in with me. I stopped working with the Sztainhorns and became David's co-worker. We settled down to married life and then it was time to begin planning for our future. David had informed his brother some time before about our marriage and I wrote about it to my sister. By my birthday, June 10, 1947, I was a married, twenty-four-year-old young woman. David had turned twenty-five the previous August.

We didn't last long in our place because Cesia made my life miserable in no time – even though she didn't grow hair on the palm of her hand because we got married! It seems that I had to pay the price for her unhappy choice of a man she didn't really like. All his money couldn't hold them together. We found another, much larger furnished room with a very cultured Polish couple and their elderly father. The new place was much closer to David's business, which made life much easier. Time went by very smoothly – I organized my schedule for housekeeping and cooking and had no problems with it. We accumulated a lot of household items such as goose-down covers, linens, towels, nice silverware and dishes. David also bought me a black Persian lamb fur coat and a few nice pieces of jewellery. We both acquired a lot of beautiful, custom-made clothes. I think that I, for one, wanted to make up for all those years when I had had nothing to wear.

Even before the wedding, David had started seriously planning our immigration to Canada, our final destination. His brother had sent us various papers to fill out in preparation for our arrival. The process would apparently take a long time and we were told that we had to be patient. Some good friends of ours in Warsaw who had high positions in the Polish government advised us to go to Germany, as most of the Jewish survivors were doing. They told us that it would be easier to connect with the Canadian immigration officials there and get all the necessary papers processed much faster than in Poland. We didn't pay any attention – why should we run again? We wanted to leave properly this time, with our luggage, by airplane, like normal people. It would only be a matter of time before everything was approved, we said. In the meantime, we weren't living so badly in Lodz.

Most of our friends took the illegal route right from the beginning. They got assistance beforehand from various organizations. After a few visits from her Frenchman, Yanka also left for France to marry him. He turned out to be a very nice person. I received a few letters from her before I left myself. On the advice of her sister in Brazil, Rose Sztainhorn decided to immigrate to Palestine because Bela would be able to help them out financially there. She began preparing to leave with her brother Abraham. Henry and his wife, Bronka, remained in Lodz. I don't know why.

When people who were very close to us started leaving, we began to feel alarmed and a new kind of fear set in. But then in the summer the happy day arrived – we received a notice from the Canadian immigration authorities dated June 1947 that our visa to enter Canada would be granted. All we needed now were Polish passports. That's when our real ordeal began. The Polish officials in Warsaw kept stalling by asking us for more information and more interviews. There were always more papers to fill out and it felt endless. By the end of 1947, David's brother was furious; he couldn't understand why it was taking so long for us to get our passports. He had never dealt with a Communist bureaucracy and couldn't understand the delay. It sounded as if he was blaming us for the problems. We knew that nobody was allowed to leave the Soviet Union, but this was Poland – we found it difficult to accept the fact that now there wasn't any difference between the two regimes. The constant waiting for news from Warsaw and the many trips we took there put a heavy strain on both of us.

Over the course of 1947, we had been hearing that it was getting much more difficult to cross the border; this was another reality of life in this new "closed society." A year went by and we still hadn't received the passports. Finally, in June 1948, we got the news that we had been refused a permit to leave the country because of David's age – he was still eligible to be drafted into the army – and that was it. To say that we were disappointed is putting it mildly; we were furious, enraged and, finally, bitter. David's brother couldn't believe it and said he was going to write to the Polish government. We told him not to be ridiculous; he had no idea how this system worked.

The Polish Communist Party was consolidating their power in Poland, which had an effect on everyone's lives. The regime was becoming more and more oppressive and aggressive, very much like the government in the Soviet Union. It was only a matter of time before they clamped down on personal freedoms in all areas. We knew that we were in trouble. It was too late for us to register to go to Israel as many people had done. Rose was among the very few people we knew who managed to get permission to legally immigrate to Israel in 1948. She left after the declaration by the United Nations of the historic establishment of the State of Israel in May 1948. But we couldn't go anywhere – we had been refused exit, period. David and I were growing increasingly bitter at the Polish government. We were furious, but the same time very helpless.

We started to look for another solution. We began inquiring about being smuggled out, but for months we couldn't find anybody who could help us. By this time, everyone knew that it was almost impossible to cross the border without risking your life. Ironically, I had risked my life to get out of the country of my birth ten years before and now I was in the same position again. I knew the same thing as I had then – that nothing in the world would keep me here. It was just the same as when I had refused to marry Levan and stay in the Soviet Union. I wasn't ready to spend my life in what I called a prison without bars.

Fortunately, our relationship strengthened with our difficulties – we knew that we only had each other to depend on. We acted in total unison right from the beginning of our marriage. We respected each other's opinions, even though a resolution sometimes only came with long debates. We were both articulate and communicated very well. But the atmosphere was rather serious and heavy at times. David started to economize so we could save some money – we knew that we would need a lot to pay for a smuggler. David took trips to different places on the border to try to find someone willing to help us, without any results. Everything had to be done in total secrecy, which made our task even harder.

One day we had an unexpected visitor – my schoolmate from Zduńska Wola, Berzek Lemberg. His father, Dr. Yaakov Lemberg, had been the most respected doctor in our town and was also an ardent Zionist, head of the General Zionist organization in our town and very active in the international Zionist movement. Berzek was one of my former schoolmates in the group I had met when I first arrived in Lodz. I'd gone out with him a few times, but to me he was just another boy. He was the spitting image of his father, physically and otherwise – his father had been known in our town as a rather active "ladies' man." Berzek was just the opposite of David; he was very gregarious, self-assured and handsome, but too aggressive for me. In other words, he was a flirt. I didn't see any other side to him, I must admit, and wouldn't give him a chance. During that period – before David came back from the Soviet Union – Berzek kept disappearing, coming and going for weeks at a time and I would always wonder where he had been.

The group of people Berzek was with had left a long time ago and I wondered why he had suddenly re-appeared. He said that he had come to say goodbye – he had met David and liked him a lot – but he also unravelled the mystery of his disappearances. It turned out that he was in charge of directing a big underground organization that helped Jewish survivors reach Palestine by whatever means required, from anywhere in Europe.

He was now legally immigrating to Israel with his mother and sister, who were waiting for him in Italy. I don't know how his mother and sister survived the Holocaust. He also told me the story, now legendary, about his father, who had been made president of the Jewish council, or Judenrat, in the Zduńska Wola ghetto. The Germans had picked him to be the Jewish representative to whom they would transmit orders related to the Jews, which had to be strictly carried out. It was a job that no one envied. When the liquidation of the ghetto was imminent, the Germans asked Dr. Lemberg to make up a list of all the old, the sick and the young children. Although he didn't know exactly what would happen to them, he had heard rumours about death camps, and he agonized over the decision. The Germans told him that these people would be sent to another place where it would be peaceful and quiet. He didn't believe them, of course, and he couldn't do it. After a few days of torturing himself and his family, he made his decision: he refused.

On the day of the liquidation of the ghetto in August 1942, Dr. Lemberg was taken off the deportation train and taken to an unknown destination; some reports say that he was killed in the cemetery. Dr. Lemberg became a national hero for world Jewry after the war. He is mentioned in many books that deal with the Holocaust.

When Berzek Lemberg said his final goodbye to us in Lodz, I said to him in Hebrew, "Next year in Jerusalem," a phrase that is recited at the end of the Passover seder and the Yom Kippur service. In the diaspora it is used to express hope, literally and figuratively, for the future – the hope to meet again in the Jewish homeland, in the city of peace. At that time, I had no idea where fate would take me. He warned us about the dangers of trying to get out of Poland illegally. We should reconsider it very carefully, he said, as he knew only too well what it entailed. But we didn't give up and kept on the same course.

I met Berzek again in Tel Aviv in 1973 when I was there alone after David died. I spent a lot of time with him and his wife. After his arrival he first worked in the Israeli Intelligence Services and later in the diplomatic corps in one capacity or another all over the world. I hardly recognized him – his English was perfect and he now appeared to be a very intelligent, serious man dedicated to his country. But he was still the same flirt and tried to meet me alone, without his wife, which I very diplomatically avoided. One year after I saw him in Israel, in 1974, he died of a heart attack, just three years after David's death. He was fifty-one years old. Like his father, he died after serving his people wholeheartedly, with total commitment.

~

In mid-1948, Rose was getting ready to leave Poland, which was very painful for her and for us. She offered to take some of our belongings with her to Israel and send them to us when we arrived in Canada. I was mainly concerned about my photographs – from home, from the Soviet Union and from the few years after the war in Poland – and various letters, including some of the postcards I had received from my parents during the war. We packed it all up, keeping just enough to put in a knapsack.

As I've said, we had beautiful clothes and Italian shoes and bags but truly, it didn't bother me too much to think of leaving everything behind. I was used to being without. I knew from the beginning that our lifestyle in Lodz after the war would be temporary and I was right.

We couldn't afford to indulge in any negative thinking. We had to concentrate only on getting out. Some friends of ours suggested that we go to Szczecin, a port on the Oder River that, by way of a system of waterways, led to Berlin. They had some friends living there and would write them to ask them to give us assistance. Once we were there, we hoped to find smugglers to take us to Berlin and into one of the western zones.

At least now we had some framework of action, something to hang on to. David started slowly selling off and not buying any more raw materials, trying to get out as much cash as possible. We had to be very careful that our workers and our landlord didn't suspect anything. It was nerve-wracking, but what else could we do? We wrote to David's brother, telling him our plans and letting him know that if we were lucky to arrive in the American-occupied western zone of Germany, we wouldn't have any means of supporting ourselves. He promised, without any hesitation, to look after us. All we would need was food and shelter until we could find a way to get to Canada. We also wrote to my sister, who intended to leave Marburg for Israel in May 1949. Now we also had a timeline to aim for, providing our plan worked: I very much wanted to see my sister before she left. God knew when we would meet again.

The winter of 1948 was approaching fast and our plan to leave Lodz was proceeding on schedule. All we had to do now was set a date and just disappear. A few of our friends knew about it, like the Kruks, David's ex-landlords, and a couple from Warsaw. The stage was set. It was December 31, 1948. We made arrangements with some people to go to a New Year's Eve party in a public place, where everybody would see us.

Our knapsacks were packed beforehand and we put them in suitcases so they wouldn't look suspicious – the suitcases made it look as if we were going for a regular trip. We came home, changed into our travelling clothes, picked up our suitcases, left everything in the room untouched and went to the railway station. The one person we trusted completely was the superintendent of the building where our business was, who also worked for us. He was a very plain, good person – a Polish man with a wife and a young son. We said goodbye to him. This was our last trip out of Poland.

Finding a Smuggler

The next morning, January 1, 1949, we arrived in Szczecin and found the people who had been recommended to us, a couple by the name of Katz who had two young children and older parents. The Katz's treated us with a lot of compassion, gave us a place to sleep, fed us and tried to put us in touch with the right individuals. This unfortunately took a long time. Our nerves were shattered – we were in their place illegally and Szczecin was a port city crawling with Polish and Soviet police and authorities. Everyone was supposed to register where they were staying, even if it was for just one night – this rule was the same as in the Soviet Union. If a neighbour were to see strangers for a prolonged period of time, they would very likely inform the police. Because of this, our friends had to find us a new place to hide out and we rented a room nearby. We tried not to go out much during the day so as not to be noticed. The days dragged on. We tried to control our emotions and not to get at each other, but it was difficult sometimes.

After a very long two months, we finally got in touch with someone who connected us to smugglers. We were given the address of an ordinary small private house. We arrived there one evening and met two Jewish men who were maybe in their thirties and very business-like – they didn't use any extra words. They presented us with the following proposition: They knew the captain of one of the barges used for transporting mineral salts from Szczecin along the Oder River to

Berlin. The captain had been in the German navy and had been taken prisoner by the Soviets. These two Jewish men had used these barges to smuggle out thousands of people, but this was some time ago. The situation was completely different now because the Communist regime had tightened border security and so it was much more dangerous. It was up to us whether we wanted to risk it; they couldn't guarantee anything. If we decided to embark on this trip, they would direct all our moves from now on and communicate with the captain, whom we wouldn't meet until we got on the boat. The German captain and his crew were risking just as much as we were, or even more. We listened, without asking any questions.

Then they raised the all-important issue – money. The amount that they asked for was astronomical; we simply didn't have that much. We told them the truth, but they didn't believe us and sent us away. We were devastated and I began to feel guilty for having spent so much money on clothes. But we didn't know then that we would be facing such a dilemma. I said to David, "Let's go back. We can't return to Lodz, but we could go to Warsaw and live like everybody else." I was tired of all the stress by now and resignation had set in. David wouldn't hear of it. He got in touch with the two Jewish men again by himself and persuaded them that we didn't have any more money. These people were mercenary, trying to get every last penny out of us. It was strictly a business for them; they didn't actually care about helping anyone. We found out later that they had used us as guinea pigs – this was actually the first voyage they had arranged with this captain on that route.

After David struck the deal, we were given all the details of the escape and the whole itinerary. We would start out on a bus as part of a group of four people – the two of us and two other young men we wouldn't meet until the very last moment. We were to act as if we were strangers on the bus but we had to get off at the same stop and try not to lose each other. We were given very detailed directions to memorize and were cautioned not to look suspicious or behave in any way that would attract attention. The more I heard, the more hor-rified I became. I already couldn't sleep at night; I was scared to death.

At a designated spot, they continued, we would see a very tall man – he was the German captain. We were not to approach him, but were only to follow him, separately; each one of us would be alone, trying to follow the one in front, at some distance. We didn't know how long this walk would take or where we were going. All we knew is that we would be in the Port Zone of Szeczin, which was absolutely forbidden for regular civilians. We would be heading to a spot where a rowboat would be waiting to take us over to the barge. We were told that if the port police saw us, well, good luck to us. The captain supposedly knew what he was doing so we would probably be okay. After all, he didn't want to be caught either.

All we could do was wait for the designated time of departure, which would be the first cloudy night. As if to spite us, the sky was as blue and clear every night as it was during the day. I became very depressed, seeing the hand of destiny at work once again, as it had been so many times before.

This whole episode reminded me so much of the period before I left my family and the process of escaping from Poland. Now, how-ever, it was even worse – now we knew the Soviets and what to expect from them. I hadn't been the master of my fate when I left Poland the first time and I wasn't now. But there was no time for panic. We tried to psyche ourselves into being ready for this "adventure," because there was no way out of it – we had given the smugglers the money in advance. Our friends in Szczecin told us this was the normal proce-dure. Every night we looked at the sky, not for the stars, God forbid. This torture went on almost to the end of March 1949.

The moment finally came. We got the signal and started out. Sitting on the bus with David as though he was a stranger was already enough for me. I was petrified – what if I got off too early or too late? I hoped that nobody could see the fright on my face. Getting off at the same stop worked fine. I saw David walking and followed him, not paying attention to the other two boys. They were supposed to get on another boat in the same chain of six. Suddenly I saw a towering figure, probably six foot six, standing on a street corner. Our walk began. The areas we passed through were all in ruins from bombing; there were giant holes and a lot of debris. How in heaven would I follow a man who had legs as long as I was tall and walked very fast? I was wearing little wedge sandals and my knapsack felt as if it was filled with stones. I kept falling down and getting up again, thinking, this one, I will not survive. Poor David couldn't even help me – his only purpose was to not lose sight of the giant.

I think we walked for about half an hour or more when suddenly we came to a crossroad and I lost sight of everyone. Which way was I supposed to go? Left or right? There was no time to think; we had been told in no uncertain terms that they wouldn't wait if anyone got lost. In the seconds it took me to decide, I could see in my mind's eye all the consequences: the police would find me, interrogate me, probably torture me and I would tell them everything, pull in everybody. But as I have said many, many times before, I believe in fate – I took one step and then another and, to my delirious joy, I saw them all. At that instant, standing at the crossroad, I realized that in the most difficult moments in life, everyone is alone. I had the same feeling when I was trapped on those train tracks facing the oncoming train in Małkinia.

When we reached the riverbank I was able to see the features of our "guiding light." Without speaking, he motioned everyone over to the rowboat about two or three hundred feet away. Without any hesitation, we all walked into the icy cold water that was up to our knees and climbed onto the boat. The tension was so great you could cut it with a knife.

We arrived at the first barge and David and I got off; they took the other two boys to the boat next to us. We went down to a small, dirty little cabin. It was dark, but I could see two beds, a table and chairs, and a woodburning stove. On one bed I saw a young German girl who was obviously there to keep the captain company and satisfy his needs. We were soaking wet and tried to dry ourselves in front of the stove. A big German guy came into the cabin. He completely disregarded us at first, but then started drinking and loosened up a bit. I'm sure that he was also under great tension until we arrived at our destination. The captain gave us some food, which the girl had cooked. I looked over at David and saw that he was all flushed. I touched his forehead – it was very warm. I took his temperature and saw that he was running a fever of 40 degrees Celsius. I got really scared. What could we do about it there? There was no medical help. I told the big German about it (he spoke Polish and Russian), but he just shrugged it off.

They offered us drinks and, to my great surprise, David drank the 100-proof spirits straight, and quite a bit of it. The big guy was very impressed – he tried to do it himself and couldn't. David told me later he had wanted to show this tough, dangerous individual that he was not a weak little boy. As the evening went on the German told us stories about how some friends of his had smuggled some rich Jews out of Poland on these boats, taken all their jewellery and American dollars, hung a big stone around their necks and pushed them into the water. Why did he tell us that story? Obviously, he wanted to scare us and most probably thought we also had jewellery and American money. From that moment on, we felt constant fear, expecting the worse. He gave us a cubicle next to his cabin with a wooden platform covered with straw to sleep on. It was so narrow that we had to lie on our sides and literally fit into each other. We slept in our clothes, waiting for him to come in any minute. David managed to find a big iron crowbar in the darkness and kept it in his hand while we lay there.

The first night we didn't sleep at all and fortunately it passed without any incident. During the day, the man allowed us to stay in his cabin. We hadn't yet started moving because they hadn't finished loading up the barge. We ended up staying docked in the port for a few days. The captain disappeared for hours at a time and the girl was much nicer when he was gone, giving us more food. We didn't know how long the journey would take. The distance was altogether about ninety kilometres, but the barges travelled very slowly.

We finally started moving. The German told us that when we crossed the border between Poland and Soviet-occupied Germany, a Polish patrol would come on board to look for people being smuggled out. The night before we were to reach the border, he would take us to a hiding place down below in the barge. We couldn't figure out what he was talking about. When night fell he said, "Let's go." It was very dark and I couldn't see very well because of the night blindness I acquired in the Arkhangelsk labour camp. The passageway along the edge of the boat was no more than forty-five centimetres wide and I found it very difficult to keep my balance. There was no rail or anything to hold on to and I was afraid that I would fall into the water. Miraculously, I made it. We went down some dark steps into a pit filled with mineral salts. A little higher up, like a gallery, there were some storage areas for tools. One of them had a double wall with a space between that was no more than half a metre wide by one metre long. The captain opened some boards and we squeezed inside. He closed the boards behind us and said, "Don't talk. Don't sneeze. Don't cough." (He might just as well have said don't breathe.) "If they find you, I am in even bigger trouble than you – remember that." My reaction was to think that he was better off getting rid of us after he got all the money and jewellery that he thought we had. But for once we were fortunate not to have any, and he had to have some proof that he had delivered us to get his share of our money from the smugglers.

I smoked at the time and always had a little cough. David's feet kept freezing, a problem he had had since Arkhangelsk. We were standing up in that tiny space for a few hours until at last we heard voices speaking in Polish. The guard patrol was here. I had a tremendous urge to cough – David saw it and pressed his hand over my mouth and nose so hard that I thought he would choke me. I couldn't breathe and in that instant I thought, What a way to die. But the patrol left and we survived the first test. By the time the captain came to get us we were so numb from being squeezed in for so long we could barely walk, but he kept rushing us forward like animals. When we arrived at the cabin, I began to scream hysterically. Even the captain and the girl got scared. David was perplexed at seeing me like that and just held me like a little wounded child. I eventually calmed down but was so tired that I couldn't utter a word.

That same evening, the captain began questioning us about money. We knew this would happen. He said if we had any, we had better give it to him just in case. What this "just in case" meant, we didn't dare to ask. We told him that we didn't have any and he left us alone. This was only the first grilling. We went back to our cubicle, where David put one arm around me and held the iron bar in his other hand.

We had plenty of time to think while we were on the boat, but we didn't share our thoughts in these tense moments. I was afraid to admit my fears, to look into the depths of this abyss. Although we both wanted to be hopeful, to reassure each other, submerged within each of us was the thought that perhaps this was the end of the road. Trembling with fear and cold, I reviewed my life at just twenty-four years of age, examining which of my dreams and hopes had been either realized or abandoned. I was saddened by the memory of some of my disappointments, some of the heavy losses I had experienced. In my darkest moments I thought destiny was playing with me again. I worried that I was faced with only two alternatives: that the captain would push me into the dark, cold water or that the Soviets would catch me and send me away. In either case, I would just disappear and perish like my family – "Place or Date of Death Unknown." Which one of these morbid choices would it be? David and I often looked at each other, frightened and bewildered. It was so strange, as though our emotional wiring had gone awry and all our communications had to be extrasensory.

It took another three days of slow moving before we arrived at the checkpoint between Soviet-occupied Germany and Berlin and the captain told us this inspection would be even worse. Again we were marched along the narrow path down to our hiding place. This time I could clearly hear voices in Russian saying, "Where are they, the bastards? Plenty of them got out." They poked around for a few minutes and left. The captain came to get us out again and this time I didn't cry. We had crossed through two border patrols and I thought that this would be the worst part of our ordeal. But after a couple more days, our captain told us that he had just received instructions to unload in a place just east of Berlin and go straight back to pick up another load. He couldn't drop us off in the Soviet-controlled part of Germany; we would have to stay on board until he could take us right into Berlin. From there we would cross the river to the west side of Berlin, to the American Zone. We didn't understand what he was saying, but we knew that we were at his mercy. So back we went, all the way back to Szczecin, but at least we didn't have to go through the checkpoints on the way back. They were only worried about people being smuggled out, not in.

Meanwhile, the captain was putting increasing pressure on us to give him money. He didn't believe that we didn't have any. It was clear that he didn't want to resort to violence – yet – though we didn't know why. Instead, he stopped giving us any food. From the cubicle where he kept us most of the time we could smell delicious fried potatoes, eggs, bacon and ham. Fortunately, David, being very practical, had brought a few big blocks of chocolate and this helped us get through the next few days. He rationed it, giving each of us only a couple of squares at each meal, so it would last longer. No matter how much I begged for more, he wouldn't give in to me.

I guess by now the captain believed that we didn't have any more money and it didn't pay for him to kill us. Since he hadn't been paid yet, we were worth more to him alive. He started giving us bread and his girlfriend let us have some other food when he was out.

We started our trip all over again, going through the same patrol stations, but for some reason, the barge wasn't searched again. At long last, we arrived in the Soviet zone of Berlin. We had been on the boat for twelve days but the worst two days were actually ahead of us. We could see Soviet motorboats zipping along the river every few minutes, many of them, back and forth. We could also see across to the other bank of the river, maybe 300 or 450 metres away at this point, where our freedom was waiting for us, so close and yet so far.

The water near the bank where the boat was docked was frozen and the waterway was only thawed in the middle. How was the captain going to get us onto the paddleboat and across fast enough in between the speeding Soviet patrol boats? This was the first time he had ever tried this and we could see that he was very nervous. After two days he and his crew got us into the small paddleboat and we prayed that God would help us all.

The timing had to be perfect and we would be very lucky to make it across. To our horror, however, we could see that on this side the water quite a distance from the bank was frozen solid. I had never seen two men chipping away ice with plain wooden paddles with such speed. I had never seen the strength that fear could produce.

As soon as we got to the other bank we jumped out, didn't say goodbye, and found ourselves, almost delirious, on solid ground. We hadn't even taken it all in yet, comprehending what had taken place and where we were. We started walking away from the river, taking care not to move too fast, so we wouldn't look suspicious. Although it wasn't necessary anymore, we still wanted to be careful. We saw a sign with the name of the street that our contacts in Szczecin had given us. There were people waiting for us in the American-occupied zone of west Berlin, a couple who we would be able to stay with for a few days. We finally began to realize that we had made it, but we didn't dare talk out loud yet. I kept whispering for the longest time. I learned then, more than ever before, that freedom shouldn't be taken for granted.

Starting Over

After our dramatic escape from Poland and our arrival in Berlin, we went on to Marburg. At last, I would see my sister Fela again. I recorded most of what happened after that in letters to my friend Rose in Israel, so I am using excerpts from these to describe the rest of my journey. The last time I had seen Rose was in 1948. Twenty-five years later, in 1973, I met her in Tel Aviv and we exchanged all the letters we had written to each other.

The letters, written in Polish, are now about forty years old, yellow and brittle like autumn leaves. I still have them all in my possession. I decided to use some excerpts from them, translated into English, because they describe the events better than my memory could possibly recall.

~

July 25, 1949, Marburg
Dear Rose,

We rented a room from a German woman and got our stuff in order. We had a rest and started organizing our next plan, to get to my sister, Fela, who lives in the American Zone. As you know, Berlin is occupied by four nations: France, Britain, the United States and the Soviet Union, and when we were there it was blockaded by the Soviet army. The Joint [American Jewish Joint Distribution Committee], *a Jewish international organization, took care of us by giving us food and offering shelter, which we didn't need. We told them we were going to Israel (this was the only way they could get us out) and they took care of all the necessary documentation. We got a travel document with a visa to Israel and after a couple of weeks we flew to Frankfurt, ninety kilometres from Marburg, where my sister lives. By the way, this was my first voyage on an airplane. On April 8, 1949, we arrived at my sister's place.*

The joy of seeing each other was so great that we could barely stop talking. Unfortunately, Fela had already made all her arrangements to go to Israel and she left after four weeks. We parted again and God knows for how long. As a matter of fact I just received a letter from her. She writes that life in Israel is very hard, that she can only dream about getting a flat of her own, and that there is a lot of unemployment. So in the meantime she is living with our brother in his three-room flat. It must be very crowded with six people. My sister-in-law just gave birth to another girl. Fela writes that Mordechai hasn't been too lucky either, and that even after so many years in the country, he is still not doing too well financially. He is working as an electrical mechanic in an army hospital. He can't support his family on his salary and he especially can't afford education for his older daughter, who is fifteen. His wife has to work at home as a hairdresser since she also has a baby to look after. Is it really true, Rose, what my sister writes about Israel? That you can see luxuries next to extreme poverty?

As for us, after my sister left we remained in her nicely furnished two-room flat (that we rented). The town is beautiful and has a river running through it. It is surrounded by mountains and is very picturesque. It's like a health resort and is even nicer than Kudowa-Zdrój. You can get everything here, although food is very expensive, and there is cloth that we haven't seen in Poland in such a long time. All you need is money, and this we are short of. David's brother cannot send us any directly from Canada, so we found a contact in New York to go through, but we still don't have enough to live on. We could have lived well on this amount in Poland, but here the dollar isn't worth as much.

We were forced to sell our good Leica camera. We are often upset about this constant penny-pinching, as we weren't used to it in Poland. Lately I have become so economical, you wouldn't believe it.

Anyway, I'd better get used to it. In Poland the conditions were totally different and now I must worry more about the future. We have to start from scratch. Imagine, I have hardly anything to wear! Since I left in the winter, I didn't take much to begin with, but I didn't bring any summer clothes at all. It's hot, so I bought just one little cotton dress and this is what I have to wear all the time. I don't have the money to buy anything else and David's brother writes that we will get clothes in Canada. My sister can't send me any of her clothes from Israel because parcels cannot be sent from Israel to Germany. From so many shmattes [clothes], I have nothing to wear.

But I don't worry about it too much. Somehow I will survive this period, and nobody knows me here anyway. The main thing is how our future in Canada will work out. As for our voyage to Canada, we are waiting to be called to the Canadian consul and doctor. After that, things will go faster. You have no idea how much we would like to be there already.

I am curious to meet David's brother, Jack, and our sister-in-law and the whole family. David's uncle from Argentina just arrived in Toronto, so the family is going to be complete. David's brother is getting married in Chicago shortly before our arrival. We couldn't have gone to Chicago anyway and her family wants it to be there. Perhaps all these little things I write about are of no interest to you, but I write them because you always knew everything about our lives, as we knew about yours.

The days here are sometimes monotonous and we feel a bit isolated, but we somehow try to fill them. We take little excursions into the mountains and other places of interest and we bought monthly tickets to the swimming pool. I am taking swimming lessons. We also play a lot of chess to pass the time.

~

August 7, 1949, Marburg
Dear Rose,

You are doing the right thing by writing about every little seemingly unimportant detail because then I can get a complete picture of your life there, almost as if I were with you. I get a strange feeling when you write about our mutual friends. I feel sad about my life going in a different direction. Lately, David is very drawn to Israel; it's too bad we don't have any money because otherwise we might be able to go where we really belong. It's too bad, but we realize that with empty hands it wouldn't be easy, even among our own people. In any case, my sister tells me not to come. Her letters are not at all positive.

What other news do you get from Poland? What is the atmosphere there? Have any Jews been able to leave Poland lately? We get some letters from there, but they seem to be very censored so we have to read between the lines. I am curious to know what plans your brother Henry has, as far as leaving Poland. We had intended to help him and it wouldn't have cost him as much as we paid. We wanted to get in touch directly with the captain of the boat that took us across. We wrote to someone in Berlin about this and we received the bad news that on the very next trip after ours, the crew and the passengers (like us) were all caught by the Soviets. I know too well what they can expect.

All in all, we haven't yet had a peaceful day in Marburg. We still have such a shortage of money to live on, which I never experienced in Lodz. We were sure that David's brother would send us money immediately, but it took six weeks until we got anything from him. We don't know anyone here we could borrow from and we have had to sell some things just to buy food.

Luckily, David's friend from Russia, Wrublewski, visited us on his way to Israel and we were able to get some money from him. But then we worried about David's brother because we hadn't gotten a letter from him for a few weeks. We thought there must have been something wrong because surely he wouldn't abandon us now, especially since he knew about how hard it was for us to escape from Poland. After a few weeks we finally received a letter from him, but it turned out just to be some legal papers, without any note. We were sure something had happened to him. We even thought that maybe he had had an accident. David was beside himself and very depressed. He couldn't sleep, couldn't eat. After all, he's his only brother. The money part didn't matter anymore, all we cared about is knowing that he is still alive. Jack has taken on a very special meaning to us. Our future is linked to him and to a new world, a new life.

We wish so much to arrive at our final destination and begin some kind of a normal life. Right now I can't even imagine it or believe it will ever happen.

After a few weeks, we finally got a letter from Jack. We were ecstatic and forgave him for leaving us without any means of support. He is alive and that is all that matters. It turned out that he was really dangerously ill. He had nose and throat surgery and then got out of the hospital too early and developed an infection with serious complications. So Jack is fine, but we still don't have any money and food is very expensive. For a very, very meagre existence, we need at least ten to fifteen dollars a week. In total we've received 150 dollars from David's brother, but a lot of it went to travelling to different places in connection with entering Canada. We tried to sell my fur coat but it's summertime now.

Last week we finished all the formalities for immigration. We were at the Canadian consulate, where we went through all the medical examinations and so on. We had some problems with the security people because the fact that we managed to get smuggled out of Poland so late, when it was almost impossible, made us look suspicious to them. They almost didn't pass us and they kept grilling us, together and separately, for hours. A few days ago, we received notice from the consulate to be ready to leave on September 6 from the city of Hamburg. The cost of the voyage by ship is covered by the Joint. Now we are very upset because we have no money and we need to buy a suitcase and my shoes are just falling apart.

We are going to have to stay in some kind of a camp, a quarantine, for two to three weeks. How can we be there without a penny? Had we known before that we would get so little support from David's brother, we could have sold my fur coat in Berlin for at least a thousand dollars, and we could have had peace of mind.

I don't know what we are going to do if the money doesn't come. Maybe we will try to sell my gold bracelet, a gift from David. But we must go and somehow we will get there. As you can see, it's not easy for us now. At least I am glad that I managed to put together a nice outfit for when I arrive in Canada.

I just want to have this all behind me. I'm very curious about our future in Canada. I don't imagine that everything will be rosy. It will be necessary "to roll up our sleeves," as we say in Polish. I'm sure I will have to go to work in order to get anywhere. It would be terrible to regret deciding to go to Canada as we've already had such a rough time getting there.

David is well and his only problem here is this long period of not doing anything. It drives him crazy. He is also very upset about me hardly having any clothes and being so unable to change anything. But he is very happy to see that I'm not losing my sense of humour and good spirits in this difficult situation. Just the opposite, I've been taking it all lightly for his sake. If, for instance, we want to go to the movies, I'll give up some food, like eggs for breakfast or meat for dinner, and it's fine.

The main thing is that everything is fine between us, as it was before – maybe even better. Since we only have each other, we are becoming even more attached to one another. Whether things are good or bad, it's the relationship that matters and the two of us are getting along beautifully. Right now, as usual, he is lying on the couch and reading. He knows German very well already. Sometimes he reads for most of the day and this helps him forget the problems we have to deal with.

At long last … Canada!

October 12, 1949, Toronto

Dear Rose,

We finally arrived at our destination, Toronto. It sounds so simple and matter of fact, but you know very well what it means to us. We arrived in Toronto on October 5, 1949. We left Marburg on September 6 and we wandered from one DP [displaced persons] camp to another until September 17, when we boarded the ship in Hamburg.

Our voyage wasn't very easy. Pretty much everyone got sick and one Jewish woman even died. We sailed on an army transport ship and had to do everything – such as cleaning and cooking – ourselves. We spent time with some Jewish people and became friends with some who were also going to Toronto, especially Elizabeth and Salek Borek.

We arrived at the port of Halifax and from there we travelled by train for two days. As I mentioned to you in my last letter, we hadn't heard anything from Jack for the last few weeks, so we were sure that no one would be waiting for us in Toronto. We had even made arrangements with Elizabeth and Salek to go with them to their brother's.

We felt very abandoned and alone. The worst moment was getting off the train and we walked slowly from the train into the station. But when we got inside, there were about twenty people waiting for us, along with David's brother! I just stood there, feeling numb and speechless, alternating between crying and laughing as I looked at this emotional scene. We drove in Jack's car to his aunt's house, a place where Jack had stayed before. She is David's father's sister. Jack told us that she is the poorest of the three sisters but also the nicest. They have seven children and five of them already have their own families. Her husband, David's uncle, is a carpenter.

I was surprised to see that this so-called poor aunt had her own ten-room villa! The first day we spent with her, relatives came and went for the entire day. It was a blur. A month before we arrived, David's father's brother came from Argentina for a visit, another aunt came from

California, and there is also another aunt here, so David now has three aunts and an uncle here.

In all, a few hundred people came to see us; it felt almost as if we were some kind of rare exhibit. First cousins with their children, second cousins, friends of our relatives, on and on it went. Jack told us that most of the relatives are well off, but we don't really understand what that means yet. In the evening, we went to sleep at the house of one of David's father's first cousins because Jack said it would be quieter for us there. She has a smaller, newer villa with all the rooms on one floor. She gave us a beautifully furnished pink bedroom to stay in until the one-room flat that Jack arranged for us is ready.

We were finally able to relax and rest up after a day of very strong impressions and emotions, and could share what we were feeling. Naturally we couldn't sleep, as we had to talk about everything. David's brother made a very good impression on me. He is elegant, very North American, sophisticated-looking and outwardly doesn't resemble David at all. I was surprised to see that his hair is already greying at the age of thirty-one, but, as we heard, he has been through a lot – he was on the front lines during the war. It is difficult to convey how happy he appears to be with our arrival. We heard from all our relatives how he has been dreaming of this reunion, which was very touching indeed.

Jack told us that he's sorry he can't help us out more and that if he was in a better financial situation he would give us much more. But he immediately gave us 1,000 dollars, which is quite a bit of money for us. He drove here from Chicago three days before our arrival and rented a room for us. He told us that lately it's been difficult to find accommodation in Toronto and it's also very expensive. He wanted us to have our own place right away, instead of staying with relatives, which made sense to us.

Jack just got married a month ago to a woman named Betty from Chicago and the wedding was very elaborate. There were two hundred guests and, just imagine – the cost of the wedding was 3,000 dollars! Betty is coming on Saturday and I'm very curious to meet her. She couldn't come earlier because she's been too busy managing her late father's leather goods factory. Jack feels bad that he'll be living in Chicago, but right now it can't be helped.

Don't be surprised, Rose, if my writing is somewhat chaotic, but there is so much I want to write about, so many interesting new things, that sometimes I don't know where to begin. I've been here for six days already and I still can't gather my thoughts. We meet new relatives, closer or further removed, every day and they all keep inviting us over for dinner – if we accepted all the invitations, we'd have to eat five dinners a day!

All the people we meet like us very much and we're making a very good impression on them. Jack is very proud of us. We are overwhelmed with the warm welcome we've received in Toronto. As for life in general here, I have to write a separate letter, but I'll tell you now that I never could have imagined that plain working people could live so well. A very average working person's house would be like a beautiful villa in Poland; you can see whole streets of them here. In general, Toronto is a beautiful city. I wonder when I will find my way around – l haven't walked anywhere yet. I admire the women I've met; they are so elegant, secure and rather sure of themselves.

Right now I am still a little mixed up and it will take a while to sort things out. As for our future, we don't know anything yet. At any rate, I will go to work, as do most women here. We'll be able to support ourselves with one salary and save the other one.

I also must tell you that when I look at the two brothers and see how happy they are together, it moves me to tears. Jack is intelligent and I think they really understand each other. They haven't had much time for personal talks because there are always so many people around. If they need to talk they have to get into the car or go to a coffee shop. Can you imagine how I feel with the two brothers? It still seems so unbelievable and unreal.

~

October 22, 1949, Toronto

Dear Rose,

I couldn't write for the last few days because it's been the Jewish holidays and there have been constant family gatherings. I am simply exhausted. Besides, Betty arrived to see us and stayed for three days. I will write about her sometime later. I received your letter today and this gave me an incentive to write you again.

Jack went back to Chicago and the two of us are alone for the first time in our own little flat. It's two o'clock now and I hope that I will finish writing by seven because one of our cousins just called and we've been invited to another cousin's house for a big reception.

Sometime I will write to you specifically about the young people that are closer to our age. There are so many interesting observations I have, but this will take too much time today.

On Tuesday evening, family members arranged a "shower" for me, which is usually the custom before you get married. There were one hundred women – relatives and their friends – and it was a "welcome to the country" reception. I received a lot of household gifts, almost everything I need. We got fifty bath towels, thirty tablecloths, bed linens, china dinner sets, tea sets, blankets and everything we need for the kitchen. They keep asking me what else I need. Today they delivered a special table with four chairs (they call it a bridge table) for playing cards. I've never played cards in my life.

As you can see, we are set for the time being. As for clothes, Jack made sure we both got plenty from some of our relatives who have manufacturing plants. He wants us to Americanize in a hurry, but I will also talk about that some other time. Everyone just adores David. Luckily I don't have to worry that they will make him conceited – David isn't like that. As for me, the phones have been ringing off the hook since my reception and I got feedback from one cousin that I looked very nice and made a good impression.

Our relatives here are from various different backgrounds, but most of them are doing very well financially. Some are very wealthy and own big businesses. Even the ones who work for others live well; most have houses and others have big apartments.

Refrigerators, washing machines and dishwashers are necessities and everybody has them. Life is much easier here in every respect and there are all the modern conveniences. Of course you have to work, but people earn enough from their work to own houses and cars. Women also work here, even the ones who have children. The children go to preschool while their mothers work during the day.

Yesterday we visited a cousin of David's father who is a tailor and has been here for twenty years. You should see how these people live! A seven-room house with all the conveniences. Their children go to school and their nineteen-year-old daughter just finished high school and works in an office now. She is a beautiful girl, tall and blond – a totally different type from what we see in Europe.

People here may be less intellectual than we are, but they are very sure of themselves. They are open and direct and, of course, this fits their way of living, which is quite different from ours. Too bad we have trouble communicating with the people our age – they speak very little Yiddish. Despite that, you have no idea how strong the Jewish spirit is among the young people and in the Jewish community in general. Most of them belong to some kind of Zionist organization and I hear all the time about various meetings, conferences and seminars. Their meetings are very different from the ones we used to have in Poland. As a matter of fact, I went with someone to one of these meetings not long ago and it more resembled a social gathering. They rent a place in a big hotel and the ladies arrive beautifully dressed. Everyone is seated around tables and someone says a few words about Israel, mostly about the money they need there. Afterward, the ladies chat with each other, smoke and play cards while the waiters serve food.

Some of the Canadians I've met think that Europe is an antiquated concept and that anyone who comes from there should throw away their old customs and Americanize instantly. They are very conceited about it. We don't want to get into any discussions on that subject right now – besides not all of them think the same way....

Last Sunday, one of our relatives picked us up for a drive around the city and explained every place we came across. Toronto is really beautiful, as I mentioned to you before, and it's filled with parks. The centre is built up high with offices and factories and the rest of the city consists of two-storey houses. There are very few rental buildings.

We visited two department stores and I was overwhelmed with how luxurious they were. I couldn't stop looking at all the gorgeous merchandise on display. I'd like to be able to come close to this type of living, but I have to have patience. This is a country of opportunities, but not right away. The ones who have it all now also went through difficulties in the beginning.

The worst part is not knowing the language. We were left alone today and couldn't find our way around the city at all. I don't know where to go for anything and we can't always drag our relatives with us. David just went to the barber, which was a whole big undertaking; how would he know what to say and how could he make them understand what he wants? My English is not good enough yet – I can talk a little bit, but what good is it if I don't understand them? Their accent is different from what I learned in Georgia and Poland. We both enrolled in night school and I hope we'll muddle through somehow.

Taking everything into consideration, we can't complain. David's brother did his best and we have a very nicely furnished place to live. After all, we had nothing when we came. It's too bad that Jack can't be with us but he said he would visit us often. He is coming back in two months for our cousin's wedding.

As for Betty, I don't know her well enough to say too much. She speaks very little Yiddish and I think she's not very talkative, period. So far there is a distance between us. She is the same height as me, more or less the same weight, thirty years old and elegant. I have a feeling that I'll have a hard time understanding her. She seems rather dry and unsentimental, but that's how a lot of young people here appear to us so far. I'll get to know her better when I can converse with her in English.

I came home today again at three o'clock in the morning, as I've done most of the time in the two weeks I've been here. My head is overloaded with so many new impressions, so many new things and situations. I've encountered a new world here. Luckily I can talk to David and share it with him. Last night there was a party at a distant cousin of David's father and the luxury I saw is something I've only seen in the movies. In front of the house were rows of beautiful cars; it's hard to describe the inside of the house, but I'll try. I was told that there were some influential people in the Jewish community among the guests. The women were dressed very beautifully and were covered with exquisite jewellery. The tables were loaded with the most exotic dishes, but I can't tell you what kind of food there was or the names of the dishes. In the so-called basement, there was a built-in bar, with tons of different alcoholic drinks, just like they have in fancy restaurants.

The guests go downstairs for drinks, some play cards and waiters walk around the whole time serving small appetizers. I must also tell you that most of those people were not born into wealth; they came to this country twenty or thirty years ago and went through hell in the beginning, practically slaving in whatever they were doing. As a matter of fact, most of them became so prosperous during the war. I looked around at everything and couldn't stop myself from thinking that I wouldn't mind having this kind of luxury, though I know I need to have patience and work hard. We met someone at the party who came to Canada just five years ago without a penny, just like us; he now has his own large business, a house and cars.

After the party, a couple we became very friendly with drove us home and made a date with us to take us to Niagara Falls, which is about a hundred kilometres from Toronto. I remember learning about the falls in school – a beautiful natural creation. I never dreamt I would see them in real life.

After nearly seven months in Canada, life had normalized and we had begun to settle down a bit. It was very difficult for David to accept the fact he would have to take any kind of work he could get and not be his own boss, but we hoped that with time things would fall into place. Although we had a lot of family here, they couldn't do much for us financially. Jack was in the process of opening a big furniture store in Chicago, but, unfortunately, he was completely dependent on Betty for money. So we found work – I worked in a relative's factory sewing railway caps and David was employed in a factory that produced kitchen tables and chairs. We both continued with these jobs for the first few months and lived in the flat on Euclid Avenue. And still there were parties….

April 1950, Toronto
Dear Rose,

Adding everything up, we can't complain about this country. We aren't much worse off than a lot of people who have lived here for many years. We have goals and we keep comparing ourselves to people who have their own big businesses and magnificent homes. I've never seen such places in my life – people have summer homes and in the winter they go to places with warmer climates, such as Florida or California.

We work during the day and we go out at night; it feels as if we lead a double life. I have never in my life been to so many parties. Any occasion is good enough to have fifty to one hundred people over: when a child is born, when a boy turns thirteen, before a wedding. You can't imagine!

I am so tired and can't wait to get home from work – then someone calls to invite us to another party. We can't refuse because it would be rude. It would have been much worse if we didn't have anywhere to go and no one paid attention to us. Before Passover, we had so many seder invitations that it was difficult to refuse some people.

As for going to work and running the household (by the way we moved to a larger two-room flat), I manage very well. There are so many modern conveniences here that make life much easier. You can call the grocery store and they'll send your order right away. I even call from work to order meats and vegetables and my groceries are there when I get home from work. You can phone a big department store for any item and they deliver it to your house. I prepare the laundry in a bundle, put it in front of the door and the cleaners bring it back nicely ironed and folded. Also, the work week is only five days here, so I have two days off.

People can live freely here and there is an open road to everything. I'm not surprised that the dollar here has such great power because you can get pretty much anything with it. I'm also not surprised that people are tempted to run after that dollar like mad.

I'm not ready yet to make any judgments on the effect this has on people's individual lives and on society. To be honest, sometimes I feel funny seeing the way some people live and what their priorities are.

I am sure that David and I will find our own value system as we go along, but for now we are observers and learners.

My letters to Rose are actually very, very long and detailed. I have only pulled out the parts that describe my very candid impressions of Canada seen through the eyes of a newcomer. I seemed to have behaved like a wide-eyed girl dropped off in wonderland.

I would also like to include one more excerpt from a letter we had received from our former Polish superintendent in January 1950:

January 27, 1950, Lodz
Dear Mr. & Mrs. Recht,

We received your parcel and letter and it made us very happy. We appreciate very much that you remember us and sent us so many good things for Christmas, as I am sure you don't have it so easy yet. We thank you for your good heart. We have been anxiously waiting for this letter because we heard that the ship you were on to Canada burned down. We were terribly upset and the only thing we looked for in the parcel was

a letter – this gave us more pleasure than anything else. Now we can put
our minds at ease and be happy for you, that your dream has come true.
Mr. Recht, now I wish for you to have the son you always talked about.

~

I didn't realize that David ever talked to anyone about wanting a son
so much. In 1951, his wish came true when our son, Chuck, was born.
I do remember very well that David wanted our second child to be a
girl and that hope also came true: our daughter, Susan, was born in
1955.

I was once again thrown into a new world full of significant
changes, but this time, the changes were like a dream. The first bit of
sunshine was coming through the clouds for me, at last.

Shortly before Chuck was born, David and I managed to buy our
first home, a two-story three-bedroom house. We lived in the kitchen
and one bedroom and rented out the rest. We sold that house about
a year after Chuck was born, in 1951 or 1952, and moved into a six-
room bungalow. We lived there until the fall of 1954 – before Susan
was born – when we sold the second house for a profit and moved to
the suburbs.

David left his factory job and went to work for an upholsterer,
where he quickly became the foreman. He almost became a partner
in the business but Jack began urging David to move to Chicago,
where Jack was still living. We had received our Canadian citizenship
papers in May 1956, so David now applied for US papers. His US
visa came through in July 1956, we sold our house and David left for
Chicago – to work with his brother, he thought – in September of that
year. The children and I continued to live in Toronto, in a two-room
basement apartment, for a few months and then travelled to Chicago
to join David the following year. Unfortunately, the business plans
between David and Jack never did work out and David found himself
having to open his own upholstery shop with very little capital. Life
there remained a struggle and so, in 1962 we returned to Toronto.

Once again, we found ourselves having to start all over again. David then built up a business as a developer and started building homes in Etobicoke, just outside Toronto. He founded his company, Richdale Construction, and I worked with him in the business as an accountant and with the architects. Over the next few years, David built a number of homes and apartments – one of his best-known buildings was the Ivory Tower at Bathurst and Steeles. It had been completed at the time of David's tragic death, but not fully occupied. I took over management of the building and began to work in mortgages and investments, which I did until my retirement.

My daughter, Susan, was only sixteen and Chuck was twenty when their father died in August 1971 – how proud David would have been of both of them. Chuck graduated from the University of Toronto in 1973 with a bachelor's degree in engineering and then was awarded a scholarship to the Massachusetts Institute of Technology (MIT), where, in 1980, he earned his PhD in electrical engineering and computer science. He is now a professor at the Worcester Institute in Boston, married with two daughters. Susan earned an undergraduate degree in independent studies at the University of Waterloo in 1977, and studied at the University of Toronto for her master's degree in educational theory in 1979. In 1982 she received a PhD in clinical psychology from the Ontario Institute for Studies in Education (OISE) in Toronto. She lives with her husband and two sons in Ottawa, where she currently works as a clinical psychologist.

I never re-married, but my life has, to say the least, been full and interesting.

Epilogue

I was nervous to read this book after spending one full year writing it. In it, I have mainly covered the first twenty-six years of my life and I don't want to change a thing. The facts are true, as are my feelings when I wrote it all down.

The emotional stress that I felt while writing this book left me very drained and kind of empty. The little girl is gone; she has left me and she is out there now, in the world. I put her together and let her go, finally.

In my memoir, I have very often written about two words: fate and destiny. They mean the same thing to me. I must apologize to the little girl in me profoundly, as I wasn't fair to myself in this particular respect. It wasn't as if I didn't do anything myself – I wasn't just a pawn, moved around by fate or destiny. Sure, there is a certain amount of good or bad luck in everyone's life, but I didn't take my blows lying down – I was the one to bring about some of the changes and I was always acting and reacting in every situation. The little girl didn't just survive because fate wanted her to survive. She was using all her inner resources and strength.

Another word I used a lot was change and this forces me to explore the meaning of the word. Change can bring about challenge, growth, commitment, involvement and control – ironically, control of the very destiny I talked about so often. If this is what it means,

I experienced it all. I used change to my best advantage, whenever possible.

Maybe it's true that pain and sorrow can be prerequisites for happiness. I certainly had enough of the former. Whether this so-called happiness ever arrived in my later years is questionable and difficult to answer.

I also must admit that after reading my own writing, I am forced to reflect on my very inner self. The new perspective I have on my past has altered my way of thinking and prompted me to re-evaluate the road I am on, the ways I deal with the world at large and people in particular.

I kept my promise to my children about some day putting my story down on paper without realizing that at the same time I accomplished something of great benefit to myself. My last remarks would have to be: the twenty-six years I have focused on were certainly very long and very loaded years. The little girl came through it all a little scarred, but still together. I am proud of her now.

Glossary

Agudath Israel (Hebrew; Union of Israel) An Orthodox, non-Zionist Jewish political movement established in Poland in 1912. In interwar Poland, it gained the support of Hasidic leaders and developed a religious following. The direction of the party in religious, social and political issues was determined by Torah scholars, who generally opposed Zionist organizations that aimed to establish secular Jewish life in pre-state Israel. *See also* Bund; General Zionism; Hasidic Judaism; and Zionist and Jewish movements in interwar Poland.

aliyah (Hebrew; pl. *aliyot*; literally, ascent) A term used by Jews and modern Israelis to refer to Jewish immigration to Israel; the term is also used to refer to "going up" to the altar in a synagogue to read from the Torah.

Allied Zones of Germany After Germany's defeat in World War II, the country was divided into four zones, each administered by one of the four major Allied powers – the United States, Britain, France and the Soviet Union. These administrative zones existed in Germany between 1945 and 1949.

American Jewish Joint Distribution Committee (JDC) Also known colloquially as the "Joint." A charitable organization that provided material support for persecuted Jews in Germany and other Nazi-occupied territories and facilitated their emigration to neutral countries such as Portugal, Turkey and China. Between 1939 and 1944, JDC officials helped close to 81,000 European Jews find asylum in various parts of the world. Between 1944 and 1947, the JDC assisted more than 100,000 refugees living in DP camps by offering retraining programs, cultural activities and financial assistance for emigration.

American Zone. *See* Allied Zones of Germany.

antisemitism Prejudice, discrimination, persecution and/or hatred against Jewish people, institutions, culture and symbols.

Arkhangelsk A northern industrial city and administrative district in the far north of Russia. The city lies more than 1,000 kilometres north of Moscow on the banks of the Northern Dvina River near where it flows into the White Sea. There were a number of gulags, or "corrective labour camps" in the Arkhangelsk district during Stalin's regime. *See also* Soviet labour camps.

ayin hora (Yiddish; evil eye) A term denoting either a look (usually of envy) that can bring bad luck to the person to whom it is directed or the power ascribed to a person who can inflict misfortune with such a look. Although the notion of the evil eye exists in many cultures, the concept among Jews is based on the discussion in the Torah that envy can often lead to negative consequences. The expression *kein ayin hora*, which literally means "there should be no evil eye," is often used to ward off this negativity.

biezhenietz (Russian; stateless; refugee) A term used to define people escaping war in their country and seeking refuge elsewhere. The word literally comes from the words meaning "without a land."

black market An illegal and often informal economic system. In the Soviet Union, with the inherent shortages and bureaucratic complexities and constraints of the Soviet economic system, many people risked participation in an underground black market to get ordinary goods and services, or informally bartered or traded within it. As a matter of everyday survival, most Soviet citizens knew how to steer through a complicated and often corrupt bureaucracy.

British Mandate Palestine The area under British rule established by the League of Nations after World War I. Currently encompassing present-day Israel, Jordan, the West Bank and the Gaza Strip, the land was administrated by the United Kingdom – which restricted Jewish immigration – between 1923 and 1948.

Bund (Yiddish; short for Algemeyner Yidisher Arbeter Bund in Lite, Polyn, un Rusland, meaning the Jewish Workers' Alliance in Lithuania, Poland and Russia) A Jewish social-democratic revolutionary movement founded in Vilnius, Lithuania in 1897 to fight for the rights of the Yiddish-speaking Jewish worker in Eastern Europe, advocate Jewish cultural autonomy in the Diaspora and champion Yiddish language and secular culture. In interwar Poland, the Bund was one of many Jewish political organizations that also had affiliated schools, youth groups and sports clubs.

Central Committee of Polish Jews (in Polish: Centralny Komitet Zydow Polsce, or CKZP) Also called the Jewish Committee. An organization established in 1944 and officially recognized as the highest administrative body of Polish Jewry, the Central Committee sought to reconstruct post-war Jewish life in Poland. Between 1944 and 1950 it received funds to finance its work caring for Jewish refugees from the Polish government, as well as from the American Jewish Joint Distribution Committee. The CKZP set up various departments to help survivors search for their families and document their testimonies. The organization also provided legal assistance, social services and health care, established orphanages, and disseminated reports and newsletters on the state of Jewish life in post-war Poland.

cohen (Hebrew; pl. *cohanim*) In biblical times, *cohen* was the word for priest. The *cohanim* were responsible for worship ceremonies in the days of the Temple in Jerusalem. In the post-biblical era, a *cohen* refers to a male Jew who can trace his ancestry to the family of Judaism's first priest, Aaron, the brother of Moses. *Cohanim* occupy a special ritual status in Judaism (such as reciting certain blessings in synagogues). According to Jewish traditions, particular rules apply to a *cohen*, such as having no contact with dead bodies and not marrying a divorcee or a convert to Judaism.

The Communist Manifesto A political text written by Karl Marx and Friedrich Engels in 1848 that explores class struggle and theorizes that capitalism will be replaced first by socialism and eventually communism.

DP camps Facilities set up by the Allied authorities and the United Nations Relief and Rehabilitation Administration (UNRRA) in October 1945 to resolve the staggering refugee crisis that arose at the end of World War II. The camps provided temporary shelter and assistance to the millions of people – not only Jews – who had been displaced from their home countries as a result of the war and helped them prepare for resettlement.

East Berlin The former capital of the German Democratic Republic (also known as East Germany). In the administrative division of Germany established by the Allies immediately following the German surrender in 1945, the city of Berlin as a whole was located in the Soviet-occupied zone, but was divided into four zones controlled by the United States, Britain, France and the Soviet Union. In 1949, the Soviet Zone in Germany became the German Democratic Republic, and the Soviet Zone in Berlin – East Berlin – became the new country's capital. East Berlin was separated from West Berlin by the Berlin Wall in 1961, which fell in 1989. In 1990, the German Democratic Republic and the Federal Republic of Germany (West Germany) were reunited. *See also* Allied Zones in Germany; West Berlin.

General Zionism Initially a term used to indicate membership in one of the nationwide sections of the Zionist Organization – later the World Zionist Organization – as opposed to any of the smaller Zionist factions with specific political affiliation. As the Zionist movement became increasingly polarized between Labour Zionism on the left and Revisionist Zionism on the right, in 1922, the non-aligned mainstream Zionists formed the Organization of General

Zionists as a centrist political party within the Zionist Organization and, after 1949 and the creation of the state of Israel, participated in elections for the Knesset, Israel's elected parliament. *See also* Zionism; Zionist and Jewish movements in interwar Poland.

Georgia A country in the Caucasus region traditionally considered the dividing line between Europe and Asia that was annexed by the Soviet Red Army in 1921 and incorporated into the Soviet Union until 1991. Joseph Stalin was an ethnic Georgian and during World War II over 700,000 Georgians fought in the Soviet Red Army against Nazi Germany. The Georgian language is distinct from Slavic languages and is the most prevalent of the South Caucasian languages, containing over fifteen different dialects. *See also* South Ossetia.

German invasion of the Soviet Union. *See* Operation Barbarossa.

ghetto A confined residential area for Jews. The term originated in Venice, Italy in 1516 with a law requiring all Jews to live on a segregated, gated island known as Ghetto Nuovo. Throughout the Middle Ages in Europe, Jews were often forcibly confined to gated Jewish neighbourhoods. During the Holocaust, the Nazis forced Jews to live in crowded and unsanitary conditions in rundown districts of cities and towns. Most ghettos in Poland were enclosed by brick walls or wooden fences with barbed wire.

gulag. *See* Soviet labour camp.

Hashomer Hatzair (Hebrew) The Youth Guard. A left-wing Zionist youth movement founded in Central Europe in 1913 to prepare young Jews to become workers and farmers, to establish kibbutzim – collective settlements – in pre-state Israel and work the land as pioneers. Before World War II, there were 70,000 Hashomer Hatzair members worldwide and many of those in Nazi-occupied territories led resistance activities in the ghettos and concentration camps or joined partisan groups in the forests of east-central Europe. It is the oldest Zionist youth movement still in existence. *See also* Zionism; kibbutz.

Hasidic Judaism (from the Hebrew word *hasid*; literally, pious) An Orthodox Jewish spiritual movement founded by Rabbi Israel ben Eliezer in eighteenth-century Poland; characterized by philosophies of mysticism and focusing on joyful prayer. This resulted in a new kind of leader who attracted disciples as opposed to the traditional rabbis who focused on the intellectual study of Jewish law. Melody and dance play an important role in Hasidic worship. There are many different sects of Hasidic Judaism, but followers of Hasidism often wear dark, conservative clothes as well as a head covering to reflect modesty and show respect to God.

hora An Israeli folk dance that is performed by a group in a circle and is traditionally danced on celebratory occasions.

Jewish Committee. *See* Central Committee of Polish Jews.

Judenrat (German; pl. *Judenräte*) Jewish Council. A group of Jewish leaders appointed by the Germans to administer and provide services to the local Jewish population under occupation and carry out German orders. The *Judenräte* appeared to be self-governing entities, but were under complete German control. The *Judenräte* faced difficult and complex moral decisions often under brutal conditions and remain a contentious subject. The chairmen had to decide whether to comply or refuse to comply with German demands. Some were killed by the Nazis for refusing, while others committed suicide. Jewish officials who advocated compliance thought that cooperation might save at least some Jews. Some who denounced resistance efforts did so because they believed that armed resistance would bring death to the entire community.

kibbutz (Hebrew) A collectively owned farm or settlement in Israel democratically governed by its members.

kolkhoz (Russian) Short for *kollektivnoe khozyaistvo*, a collective farm operated on state-owned land in the USSR. The *kolkhoz* was the dominant form of agricultural enterprise in the former Soviet Union.

Komsomol (Russian) Short form of Kommunisticheskiy Soyuz Molodyozhi, meaning Communist Union of Youth. The youth movement of the Soviet Communist Party, established in 1918 and geared toward youths between the ages of fourteen and twenty-eight. The Komsomol mainly functioned as a means of transmitting Party values to future members. Members were frequently favoured over non-members for scholarships and employment; becoming a young officer in Komsomol was often seen as a good way to rise in the ranks of the Party.

kosher (Hebrew) Fit to eat according to Jewish dietary laws. Observant Jews follow a system of rules known as *kashruth* that regulates what can be eaten, how food is prepared and how meat and poultry are slaughtered. Food is kosher when it has been deemed fit for consumption according to this system of rules. There are several foods that are forbidden, most notably pork products and shellfish.

Lodz ghetto A restricted area for Jews in the Baluty district of the Polish city of Lodz. It was the second-largest ghetto in German-occupied Eastern Europe, after the Warsaw ghetto. The ghetto was sealed off on May 1, 1940, with a population of over 160,000 Jews. Initially intended as a temporary holding place for the Jews of Lodz until they could be deported, its organizational structure served as a model for the establishment of other ghettos. It was the only ghetto in which smuggling was close to impossible because it was hermetically sealed. Most of the ghetto inhabitants worked as slave labourers in factories, primarily in the textile industry. The liquidation of the Lodz Ghetto began in the summer of 1944 with the deportation of most of its inhabitants to Chelmno or Auschwitz. The few who remained were liberated by the Soviet Red Army in January 1945. The Lodz ghetto outlasted all other ghettos in Eastern Europe.

Małkinia Górna A large village and railway junction between Warsaw and Bialystok. During World War II, it marked the border between German and Soviet-occupied Poland and many Polish Jews crossed this border to escape Nazi-occupied territory.

Molotov-Ribbentrop Pact. *See* Treaty of Non-Aggression between Germany and the USSR.

NKVD (Russian) The acronym of the Narodnyi Komissariat Vnutrennikh Del, meaning People's Commissariat for Internal Affairs. The NKVD functioned as the Soviet Union's security agency, secret police and intelligence agency from 1934 to 1954. The NKVD's Main Directorate for State Security (GUGB) was the forerunner of the Committee for State Security, better known as the KGB (acronym for Komitet Gosudarstvennoy Bezopasnosti) established in 1954. The organization's stated dual purpose was to defend the USSR from external dangers from foreign powers and to protect the Communist Party from perceived dangers within. Under Stalin, the pursuit of imagined conspiracies against the state became a central focus and the NKVD played a critical role in suppressing political dissent. *See also* Stalin, Joseph.

Occupation of Poland Germany invaded Poland on September 1, 1939, and swiftly took control of Warsaw with aerial bombardments, and of Krakow, Katowice and Tunel with the use of firebombs. On September 17, the Soviet Union occupied Eastern Poland. By September 27, Polish government leaders and thousands of Polish troops escaped to neutral Romania; by October 6, Poland had been completely occupied and divided between Germany and the Soviet Union. *See also* Sikorski-Mayski Agreement; Treaty of Non-Aggression between Germany and the USSR.

Operation Barbarossa The code name for Germany's attack on the Soviet Union during World War II. On June 22, 1941, more than 4 million Axis troops crossed the Soviet front and invaded Soviet territory in the largest military operation in history. Both sides suffered severe losses, with Soviet military casualties numbering more than 2 million and Axis military casualties approximating 800,000. Germany, though initially gaining control of much of the western Soviet Union, eventually failed in its ultimate bid to capture Moscow in the long and bitter battle.

Orthodox Judaism The set of beliefs and practices of Jews for whom the observance of Jewish law is closely connected to faith; it is characterized by strict religious observance of Jewish dietary laws, restrictions on work on the Sabbath and holidays, and a modest code of dress.

Passover One of the major festivals of the Jewish calendar, Passover takes place over eight days in the spring. One of the main observances of the holiday is to recount the story of Exodus, the Jews' flight from slavery in Egypt, at a ritual meal called a seder. The name itself refers to the fact that God "passed over" the houses of the Jews when he set about slaying the firstborn sons of Egypt as the last of the ten plagues aimed at convincing Pharaoh to free the Jews. *See also* seder.

Port Zone of Szczecin Szczecin became a commercial port in 1913 with the construction of a canal to Berlin and grew in size and importance as it became a centre for the transportation of automobile parts for the growing new industry. After World War II, Szczecin was part of the People's Republic of Poland but the port zone remained under Soviet administration. Soviet authorities were pressured to hand the port zone over to the Polish Communist Party, which took place partly in 1946 and fully in January 1955.

Rosh Hashanah (Hebrew) New Year. The autumn holiday that marks the beginning of the Jewish year and ushers in the High Holy Days. It is observed by a synagogue service that ends with blowing the *shofar* (horn), which marks the beginning of the holiday. The service is usually followed by a family dinner where sweet foods, such as apples and honey, are eaten to symbolize and celebrate a sweet new year. *See also* Yom Kippur.

Sabbath/ Shabbat (Hebrew; in Yiddish, Shabbes, Shabbos) The weekly day of rest beginning Friday at sunset and ending Saturday at sundown, ushered in by the lighting of candles on Friday night and the recitation of blessings over wine and challah (egg bread); a day of celebration as well as prayer, it is customary to eat three festive meals, attend synagogue services and refrain from doing any work or travelling.

186 LITTLE GIRL LOST

seder (Hebrew; literally, order) A ritual family meal celebrated at the beginning of the festival of Passover. *See also* Passover.

Shema Yisrael (Hebrew; "Hear, O Israel") The first two words of a section of the Torah and an extremely important prayer in Judaism. The full verse is "Hear, O Israel: the Lord is our God, the Lord is one" and refers to faith and loyalty in one God, which is the essence of Judaism. The Shema prayer comprises three verses in the Torah and observant Jews recite the Shema twice daily, morning and evening.

Sikorski-Mayski Agreement An agreement signed on July 30, 1941, between the Soviet Union and the Polish government-in-exile led by General Sikorski following the German invasion of the Soviet Union, the agreement re-established diplomatic relations between Poland and the Soviet Union. After the Treaty of Non-Aggression between Germany and the USSR was signed in 1939, Poles in Soviet territories lost their Polish citizenship and those who declined to take Soviet citizenship were considered enemies of the state and sent to harsh labour camps. The situation changed after Germany's invasion on June 22, 1941, when the Soviets sought to establish political ties with the Allies. Amnesty for Polish citizens within the Soviet Union was declared on August 12, 1941. *See also* Occupation of Poland; Operation Barbarossa; Treaty of Non-Aggression between Germany and the USSR.

South Ossetia A semi-independent state currently under partial Georgian rule that previously belonged to the Republic of Georgia. During the Soviet regime, the Ossetian language was taught in the school system, but the official languages were Russian and Georgian. Tension between Georgia and South Ossetia began escalating over South Ossetia's attempts to become a fully autonomous state in 1989 and conflict broke out in the region in 1991, 2004 and 2008. *See also* Georgia.

Soviet labour camp Also referred to as a gulag (Russian), an acronym for Glavnoe Upravlenie ispravitel'no-trudovykh Lagerei, meaning Main Administration of Corrective Labour Camps. The term refers both to the bureaucracy that operated the Soviet system of forced labour camps in the Stalin era and to the camps themselves. Gulags existed throughout the Soviet Union, but the largest camps lay in the most extreme geographical and climatic regions of the country (such as in the Arctic north, the Siberian east and the Central Asian south). Prisoners endured hard labour, violence, extreme climate, meagre food rations and unsanitary conditions, all of which resulted in high death rates. Historians estimate that from 1934 to 1953 more than a million prisoners died in Gulag camps.

Stalin, Joseph (1878–1953) The leader of the Soviet Union from 1924 until his death in 1953. Born Joseph Vissarionovich Dzhugashvili, he changed his name to Stalin (literally: man of steel) in 1903. He was a staunch supporter of Lenin, taking control of the Communist Party upon Lenin's death. Very soon after acquiring leadership of the Communist Party, Stalin ousted rivals, killed opponents in purges, and effectively established himself as a dictator. During the late 1930s, Stalin commenced "The Great Purge," during which he targeted and disposed of elements within the Communist Party that he deemed to be a threat to the stability of the Soviet Union. These purges extended to both military and civilian society, and millions of people were incarcerated or exiled to harsh labour camps. During the war and in the immediate post-war period, many Jews in Poland viewed Stalin as the leader of the country that liberated them and saved them from death at the hands of the Nazis. At the time, many people were unaware of the extent of Stalin's own murderous policies. After World War II, Stalin set up Communist governments controlled by Moscow in many Eastern European states bordering and close to the USSR.

Tashkent The capital of the Republic of Uzbekistan – formerly a part of the Soviet Union – and the largest city in central Asia. During World War II, the city became the destination for more than one million European refugees, and overcrowding and hunger was common.

tekhnikum Soviet-era technical and vocational high school. The schools were a part of the Soviet mass-education system that focused on the "special middle education" of low-level industrial managers or those going into skilled trades and technical occupations.

Treaty of Non-Aggression between Germany and the USSR The treaty that was signed on August 24, 1939, and was colloquially known as the Molotov-Ribbentrop Pact, after Soviet foreign minister Vyacheslav Molotov and German foreign minister Joachim von Ribbentrop. The main provisions of the pact stipulated that the two countries would not go to war with each other and that they would both remain neutral if either one was attacked by a third party. One of the key components of the treaty was the division of various independent countries – including Poland – into Nazi and Soviet spheres of influence and areas of occupation. The Nazis breached the pact by launching a major offensive against the Soviet Union on June 22, 1941.

West Berlin The areas of Berlin occupied by the American, British and French Allied powers in 1945. When the Soviet-occupied zone of Germany became the German Democratic Republic in 1949, the Western-controlled areas of the city – still located within the boundaries of the new Soviet-controlled state – became West Berlin and remained outside the Soviet sphere as part of the new West German state, the Federal Republic of Germany. The two sections of the city were physically separated by the Berlin Wall in 1961, which fell in 1989. In 1990, East and West Germany were reunited. *See also* Allied Zones in Germany; East Berlin.

Yiddish A language derived from Middle High German with elements of Hebrew, Aramaic, Romance and Slavic languages, and written in Hebrew characters. Spoken by Jews in east-central Europe for roughly a thousand years from the tenth century to the mid-twentieth century, it was still the most common language among European Jews until the outbreak of World War II. There are similarities between Yiddish and contemporary German.

Yom Kippur (Hebrew; literally, day of atonement) A solemn day of fasting and repentance that comes eight days after Rosh Hashanah, the Jewish New Year, and marks the end of the high holidays. *See also* Rosh Hashanah.

Zduńska Wola ghetto Formed between March and June of 1940, the ghetto crowded approximately 9,000 people, including Betty Rich's family, into a small area on the outskirts of the city. It was open and operated with strict curfew hours until September 1940, when the ghetto was sealed off and conditions worsened. Various small industries operating within the ghetto – such as a small farm, a fur factory and a straw shoe factory – helped improve the lives of the inhabitants. The ghetto was liquidated on August 24, 1942: about 1,000 people were sent to the Lodz ghetto; between 6,000 and 8,000 were deported to the Chelmno death camp; and about 500 were murdered in the town's cemetery.

Zionism A movement promoted by the Viennese Jewish journalist Theodor Herzl, who argued in his 1896 book *Der Judenstaat* (The Jewish State) that the best way to resolve the problem of antisemitism and persecution of Jews in Europe was to create an independent Jewish state in the historic Jewish homeland of Biblical Israel. Zionists also promoted the revival of Hebrew as a Jewish national language.

Zionist and Jewish movements in interwar Poland Among the significant Jewish political movements that flourished in Poland before World War II were various Zionist parties – the General Zionists; the Labour Zionists (Poale Zion); the Revisionist Zionists formed under Ze'ev Jabotinsky; and the Orthodox Religious Zionists (the Mizrachi movement) – and the entirely secular and socialist Jewish Workers' Alliance, known as the Bund. Although Zionism and Bundism were both Jewish national movements and served as Jewish political parties in interwar Poland, Zionism advocated a Jewish national homeland in the Land of Israel, while

Bundism advocated Jewish cultural autonomy in the Diaspora. A significant number of Polish Jews in the interwar years preferred to affiliate with the non-Zionist religious Orthodox party, Agudath Israel. *See also* Agudath Israel; Bund; General Zionism; Zionism.

Photographs

1 Betty Rich, then Basia Kohn, with her father, mother and younger brother before World War II. Left to right, Betty's father, Chaim Moshe; Betty at age twelve; her younger brother, Rafael; and her mother, Cyrla. Zduńska Wola, 1935.

2 Betty's sister, Fela, and their older brother Jacob. Zduńska Wola, 1937.

1 Betty's future husband, David Recht, before the war (left) with his older sister and his younger brother, Isaac. Lodz, 1936

2 David's mother and his older brother, Jack. Lodz, circa 1936.

3 David's father (seated) with Jack. Lodz, circa 1936.

1   Betty and her friends in the labour camp in northern USSR. Left to right (in
    front): Feiga from Wilno; Betty; Bluma; Lola from Warsaw; left to right (behind)
    Hela; Adela; Ala; and Lola, Hela's sister, from Kalisz. Arkhangelsk, 1940.
2   Betty (left), Hela (centre) and Feiga (right) in the labour camp. Arkhangelsk, 1941.
3   David Recht, second from the left, in the same labour camp in Arkhangelsk,
    USSR, 1941.

1

2

1 Betty with the group of Polish refugees in Staliniri, South Ossetia, circa 1942. Left
   to right (in front): Feiga, Henry Sztainhorn, Betty and Srulek Lipman; (behind)
   Abraham Sztainhorn, Lola from Kalisz, her sister Hela and Aaron Liebowicz.
2 Betty in Kutaisi, Georgia, circa 1944.

Betty looking fashionable after the war. Lodz, 1946.

1

2

1 Betty (centre) with her friends Rose Sztainhorn (left) and Yanka. Lodz, 1946.
2 A seaside holiday with friends after the war. Hela is standing second from the left;
Joseph Tenenbaum in the centre; Betty third from the right; and Feiga on the far
right. 1946.

1

2

1   Betty Rich. Lodz, 1946.

2   David Recht. Lodz, 1946.

1

2

1 Betty and David on their wedding day. Lodz, March 31, 1947.
2 Betty and David's wedding dinner party. Left to right (seated in front): Betty's
   landlady, Cesia, and her husband; another couple who shared her apartment with
   Yanka; Betty; David's landlady, Helen Kruk, and her husband; and Betty's friend
   Ruth and her husband; (standing behind) Betty's housekeeper; Henry Sztainhorn
   and his wife, Bronka; David; Yanka; Abraham Sztainhorn; and Rose.

1 Betty and David on their honeymoon in Kudowa-Zdrój. April 1947.
2 Betty in front of the hotel where they stayed during their honeymoon. Kudowa-Zdrój, April 1947.
3 Betty (left), David (centre) and Manya (right), who helped them during their escape from Poland. Szczecin, 1949.

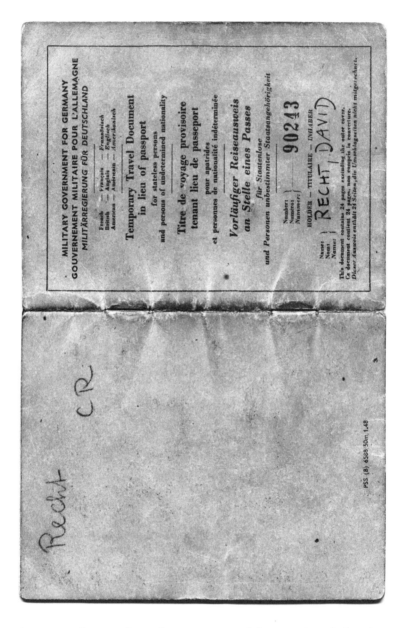

The exterior of Betty and David's temporary travel document issued when they finally arrived in the American-occupied zone of Berlin. March 1949.

The interior of the travel document.

1

2

1 Betty (left) with her sister, Fela, in Marburg, Germany, 1949.
2 Betty and David with Betty's sister and brother-in-law in Germany. Left to right:
  Betty, David, Fela and Fela's husband, Jacob. Marburg, 1949.

1

2

3
4

1 Betty, standing third from the right outside the immigration camp in Germany. Bremerhaven, 1949.

2 Betty (far left) with her luggage, preparing to leave the immigration camp. Bremerhaven, 1949.

3 Betty, far left, on the deck of the USAT *General Omar Bundy* on her way to Canada. September 1949.

4 Betty, seated on the far left, getting her first glimpses of Canada on the train from Halifax to Toronto. October 1949.

1 Betty (far left) and David (centre) with friends in Niagara Falls. 1950.
2 Betty, her son, Chuck, and David. Toronto, 1955.

1 Betty's daughter, Susan, at one year, 1956.
2 Betty's son, Chuck, at about one year, 1952.
3 Chuck and Susan, circa 1958.

Betty in Australia in 1986.

1

2

1 Betty celebrating her 80th birthday. Toronto, 2003.
2 Chuck, Betty (centre) and Susan at Betty's 80th birthday party.

Index

The Azrieli Foundation was established in 1989 to realize and extend the philanthropic vision of David J. Azrieli, C.M., C.Q., M.Arch. The Foundation's mission is to support a wide spectrum of initiatives in education and research. The Azrieli Foundation is an active supporter of programs in the fields of Jewish education, the education of architects, scientific and medical research, and education in the arts. The Azrieli Foundation's many well-known initiatives include: the Holocaust Survivor Memoirs Program, which collects, preserves, publishes and distributes the written memoirs of survivors in Canada; the Azrieli Institute for Educational Empowerment, an innovative program successfully working to keep at-risk youth in school; and the Azrieli Fellows Program, which promotes academic excellence and leadership on the graduate level at Israeli universities.